New Life

Reflections on Lent

Editors

Amy Robinson and Wendy H. Jones

DEDICATION

To all members of the Association of Christian Writers. Each and every one of you is valued, but only so many could be represented in this book. We are proud to be able to represent such a highly talented group of writers.

To Jane Clamp and Dan Cooke for their tireless help and support during the early stages of this book. Without them the book would not have come to fruition.

ACKNOWLEDGMENTS

The editors would like to thank Robert Stanek for giving up his time and using his expertise to design the cover and interior for this book. He did so without charging and for this the Association of Christian Writers is very grateful.

CONTENTS

FORWARD

Adrian Plass

The formally stated objective of the Association of Christian Writers is:

'...*to inspire Christians to use their talents and skills with integrity to write excellent material from a Christian world view'.*

As president of ACW I strongly support and agree with this aim, but after more than thirty years of battling continually with the neurotically positive defensiveness that characterises much of our modern Church, I continue to hope and pray that these words will mean exactly what they say.

'Integrity', for instance, does not come cheap. For me, being exactly what I am, and saying only what I know, is a work in progress, and a task for life. I am always ready to anatomise the hope that is in me, and to contextualise that hope, but as a writer who is also a Christian I am bound to allow struggle and resolution, disappointment and relief, doubt and faith, misery and joy and any other pair of experiential opposites to inhabit whatever I communicate, specifically Christian or otherwise. I have done my share at failing in this, but I do try.

Nobody, myself included, could possibly argue with a desire to promote the 'writing of excellent material'. However, it might be worth making one simple but crucial point. 'Integrity' is not synonymous with 'quality'. Well done, if you and I are ready and willing to communicate the truth, but neither God nor anyone else will automatically tuck 'excellent writing' into our store of skills and talents as a direct consequence. The production of worthy but unreadable Christian books and articles really is not the way to go, despite the massive deforestation that must have been required to produce mountain ranges of such publications in the past. ACW works hard to assist those members who wish to improve writing skills.

A Christian world view? Which Christians? Which part of the world? Which view? I suppose we shall only know the final answers to those questions when the very last trump dies away, and our perceptions are clarified. I am so looking forward to that day. In the meantime, I intend to store my useful personal biases and leanings carefully away ready to be used in the future, and keep a very careful eye on what Jesus actually said, as well as, perhaps even more importantly, what he did not actually say.

I am very pleased to say that the Association of Christian Writers, many of whom Bridget and I know well, are profoundly aware of the need to ensure that the aims and objectives of our excellent organisation continue to be upheld and strengthened. That is why I am pleased and privileged to offer this Foreword to a book that contains contributions from a wide variety of members, commenting on a selection of books from both Old and

New Testaments. The theme is New Life, and it is my sincere hope that, within that theme, readers will find their encounters with Scripture refreshed and perhaps even transformed.

INTRODUCTION

Angela Hobday

'New life' is a pertinent theme for the Association of Christian Writers' Lent Book which is itself a new venture. It is the brainchild of our publicity officer, Amy Robinson. Amy, together with Wendy Jones, ACW webmaster, agreed to become editors and invited members to be considered as contributors. The response was incredible, with more willing and able writers than we needed.

We, those on the ACW committee, discovered what we hoped and suspected but had never put to the test before. We are privileged to have very many brilliant writers in ACW whose faith shines through their writing. From that great pool of excellence Amy, Wendy, Janey Clamp and Dan Cooke have drawn just forty members to write a single devotional each to take us on a journey through the season of Lent.

Some of the days' meditations are very personal, illuminating parables or bible verses with illustrations from each writer's own experience. Others give us an insight and exposition of the scriptures. Entwined amongst them are thoughtful poems and prayers. Within many of the readings are challenges with questions to ponder.

Having so many contributors, the eclectic nature of the book is part of its charm. Different readers will respond to those writings which appeal to them. You may discover fresh ways of thinking or will feel stretched in your understanding, discovering new truths.

The contributions have been arranged in sections, to cover various aspects of the Christian life. They are designed to be read one day per piece. In this way there will be plenty of time to consider what has been written – but if you are more of a binge reader, you may prefer reading a few at a time. However it is approached, the variety of writing which you will encounter means it can be more than a book of readings for Lent. There is enough material within these pages to make a rich resource to mull over throughout the year.

In the words of St Paul:

I keep asking that the God of our Lord Jesus Christ, the glorious Father, may give you the Spirit of wisdom and revelation, so that you may know him better. I pray that the eyes of your heart may be enlightened in order that you may know the hope to which he has called you, the riches of his glorious inheritance in his holy people, and his incomparably great power for us who believe. Ephesians 1:17-19

So enjoy your spiritual journey with us through Lent. May the bible verses bring new life into your relationship with the Risen Lord as we travel towards celebrating the triumph of Easter.

Angela Hobday
Chair, Association of Christian Writers

Week 1:
Renewed and Restored

Introduction
Jane Clamp

At the heart of the Christian gospel is the message that what is lost may be found, what is dead may yet live. What Adam and Eve forfeited back in Eden, Jesus has restored to us: that re-connection with God that our souls crave.

Just as a master restorer would only work on an ornament that had value, Jesus invests in restoring us because He sees we are worth it! Nor does He offer only the equivalent of a spit and polish, but a thorough overhaul of our lives. The promise is not merely to improve our lives, but transform them.

We may look in the wrong places and make catastrophic decisions; but we seek the rainbow, the new song, the satisfaction of our soul. And hope underpins it all. Hope that, one day, we will find peace in our relationships, ambitions realised, our inner child healed.

Jane is creative writer in residence at BBC Radio Norfolk and on the Thought for the Day team at Premier Radio. She also preaches regularly and speaks at day conferences in which she also ministers through her saxophone playing.

Renewed and Restored
Week 1: Wednesday

Ezra 9:9

The moment I heard the yells, I snapped out of my reverie and frantically looked around. I wasn't the only one. It was a cold, wet evening in December and I was hurrying through the streets of London to catch the tube home from work. Head bowed against the wind, I was mentally reviewing my plans for the evening and not paying a great deal of attention to my surroundings. Then came the cries. I stopped. So did several others. The noise was coming from a little girl. Her mother was pulling her by the hand, no doubt desperate to get home, but the girl was resolutely pulling back and yelling, *'Mummy, look up! Look up!'*

I looked up. There, woven among the sodden trees which lined the road, were some of the largest Christmas decorations I had ever seen. Enormous illuminated snowflakes. As Christmas was just around the corner they had undoubtedly been there for some time, but here's the thing: I had never noticed them before. Not once. Why? Because I had not looked up.

It had taken someone else's cries to force me to see the bigger picture and to show me what I was missing.

Rewind 2500 years (because, in writing, you *can*) and today's reading tells a similar story. It is the cry of a man desperate for his contemporaries to stop what they are doing, look up and recognise the wonder all around them.

Firstly, let's get a little context. The book of Ezra (and big brownie points if you can find it without using your bible index) marks the end of a bleak period in Jewish history. After the glory of King David's reign, the Jewish nation steadily neglected the God they claimed to worship. They adopted pagan customs and religious practices (think child sacrifice rather than maypoles) and steadfastly refused to listen to the prophets who warned them that God would not allow such behaviour to go unpunished. Eventually things came to a head and the Babylonians invaded and conquered their land. The temple in Jerusalem was destroyed and the Jews deported to a foreign land.

Seventy years of exile went by. The Babylonian Empire was itself conquered by the Persian Empire and during the first year of the reign of the new Persian king Cyrus, an astonishing thing happened. Cyrus announced that God – incidentally not a god he worshipped – had appointed him to rebuild the temple in Jerusalem. He then added that any Jews who felt called to return home to Judah could do so. Oh, and as a fun bonus, any non-Jews living near them were to give them gold, silver and livestock to make the rebuilding possible and to enable temple sacrifices to be reinstated. I know. It's pretty unbelievable, isn't it? In fact, I think the word *miraculous* would be appropriate.

Can you imagine the reaction of the Jewish exiles when they heard the news? Disbelief? Bafflement? Utter joy? They were going home! And not escaping in fear: they were being given their freedom by the most powerful man in the land.

Slowly but surely the Jews started returning to Jerusalem where they set about rebuilding the city. There were a few hiccups (as anyone completing a building project will know) but eventually the temple was rebuilt and, in time, Ezra himself arrived with another group of exiles. As a direct descendant of Aaron, the original High Priest, Ezra was quite a Big Deal. However, his arrival was not marked by joy and celebration. The leaders of the Jewish people who had been living in Jerusalem for a while came to him with some bad news: there was a sizeable group of Jews who had engaged in intermarriage with the local people.

You can imagine Ezra's frustration, *'Are you KIDDING me? We have just been exiled for seventy YEARS because our ancestors did exactly the same thing and now, the moment we have miraculously returned home, you guys start doing it all over again? What are you? STUPID?!'*

Ezra then prayed a public prayer (which includes today's reading) in which he essentially said, *'God, you have done so much for us: you've forgiven us, restored us, brought us home and kept us safe and how do we thank you? By ignoring you and doing the very thing that caused you so much pain in the first place. Forgive us.'*

Ezra was desperate for the people to stop, look up and appreciate just how much God loved them and how much he had done for them.

I find it very easy to judge the people in this story. They were living in a time of miracles. Grace upon grace upon grace. Yet their behaviour reeked of ingratitude and apathy. How could they fail to live in awe of the God who had redeemed them?

Hmmmm. How indeed?

Today marks the beginning of Lent. A season for us to intentionally stop, take stock and remind ourselves of the God we worship. The same God who has also redeemed us from a life of slavery and oppression.

A season to remember that we too are living in a time of grace upon grace upon grace.

Perhaps today is a good day to ask yourself: am I living a thankful life, or a life of ingratitude and apathy? Have I recently reflected on all the good things God has done for me? When was the last time I intentionally opened my eyes to the wonder of God working around me?

In short: am I looking up?

Father, thank you for all that you have done, are doing and will do. Forgive me when I fail to stop and appreciate you in all your goodness. Help me to live today with my eyes wide open to who you are and how much you love me. Amen.

BEKAH FAIRLEY

Bekah studied Theology at the University of Cambridge. After graduating she worked for several churches, most recently as a Student Pastor where she spent much of her time telling very intelligent eighteen-year-olds to sleep and eat more. She now looks after her two children and blogs about her crazy life, theology and why Christians need to be more concerned about the environment. Visit her at bekahfairley.wordpress.com.

Renewed and Restored
Week 1: Thursday

Psalm 71:20

Sarah stood motionless on the hotel balcony. The night-time view was not as she last remembered it on her honeymoon. There was not the shimmer of the moonlit sky nor the winking of the stars above the shadow of the rolling hills. Tonight, instead, the aftermath of a storm lingered in the air and all was black and oppressive as she peered over the rail into the dark void fifteen storeys below.

It was here, blessed by God, she and Paul had looked out and imagined a future of promised happiness. All that was a lifetime away as miscarriage after miscarriage crushed the dream. For a moment, a few months ago, she believed her prayers had been answered but now that hope was fading. Why had God deserted her again?

A crying from inside startled her. She wrapped her dressing-gown closer and stepped back into the room. She hurried over to the wardrobe drawer pulled out onto the carpet.

Picking up the tiny bundle within, she rocked back and forth to quieten him lest someone should hear and wonder why a baby was in the room. She'd smuggled her little Matthew in sometime after she'd checked in last evening.

'There, there, my baby…Mummy's here.'

She made cooing noises as he latched onto her breast. He sucked greedily and before long, his hunger satisfied, he fell asleep. The sweet fragrance of him overwhelmed her as she lowered him into his makeshift cot.

Paul would have visited the hospital by now and reported her missing, and soon after, the nurses would have found Matthew missing too. They'd be looking for them both. Despite a stressful pregnancy this time she'd gone full term, but when the doctor took Paul aside and she'd overheard the words 'depression' and something about her needing 'psychiatric care', she'd feared they'd take Matthew away.

Paul might guess she'd come here: she had talked of it often as the last place she could remember being happy.

Exhausted, she fell back on the bed. A piercing pain in her head throbbed relentlessly. She clutched a pillow and sobbed herself to sleep.

A knocking on the door woke her. Her first frightened thought was that they'd found her.

She looked at the clock. It was morning. She opened the door a little. It was the foreign hotel maid she'd spoken to in reception when she arrived.

'Please Madam, I come to change the towels and the bed to make.'

Sarah thought quickly.

'Give me the clean towels and I'll bring the dirty ones.'

She snatched the towels and closed the door. She returned with the dirty ones and thrust them at the maid.

The maid didn't move. 'I must come in the bed to make,' she said.

Sarah waved her away. 'There's no need. It's fine.'

She refastened the door and leant back against it. She tried to think clearly but her thoughts churned into one another.

She went to the balcony window and opened the curtain. The storm had given way to a thick mist. She must get dressed, she thought. She must leave today.

When she returned from the bathroom Matthew was grizzling. She tried to feed him again but this time he turned his head away. She walked the room trying to calm him but now he was screaming. His face was bright red. Suddenly, she was aware she was slamming him up and down on the bed. What was she doing?

Trembling she left him screaming and rushed to the balcony. She felt sick. They were sure to find her. They would take Matthew away and put her in some mental institution. She looked down. How easy it would be to lean over, raise her legs and let go. All her troubles would be over. She leaned forward...the sudden ringing of the room telephone made her pause. Matthew had grown quiet. She moved back into the room and cautiously picked up the receiver but didn't speak.

'Hello!'

It was Paul.

'Sarah darling, answer me. I know it's you. Are you okay?'

'Yes. But please go away.'

'I can't do that my love. You need help. Is the baby all right?'

'Of course he is. I wouldn't harm him.'

Matthew began screaming again. She dropped the phone and picked him up. As she stared at his screwed-up face the fog in her mind cleared. He was screaming for his mother and instinctively he knew it wasn't her.

This wasn't Matthew. She remembered...her Matthew had died at the moment of his birth.

She fell to her knees, the baby in her arms. She howled in despair, 'What have I done? Oh Jesus come...please come...please rescue me.'

The door burst open. It was Paul with a policewoman.

He raced forwards and prised the baby from her. As he turned to give it to the policewoman, Sarah ran onto the balcony.

'No!'

Paul yelled and catching her arm at the last moment he dragged her back from the rail. He held her close, her body shaking with inconsolable grief.

Paul gently turned her face to look out. The sun had burnt off the mist. She could see the lush green of the hills flecked with little white dots of sheep. Against the backdrop of a blue sky, an arched rainbow had sprung from the depths of the earth to the heavens above. The pain in her head faded as the feeling of God's presence surrounded her.

Paul kissed her and whispered, 'It'll be all right. Children or no children things will get better my love. Grip my hand and hold on. I promise you, in our dreams we'll walk those hills together again and we'll sing the new song God has in store for us.'

The rainbow glowed brighter and she felt God's love strengthen her for the journey ahead.

BRIAN VINCENT

Brian began writing with sketches to illustrate church sermons and 'Daily Thoughts' on local radio. This developed into writing articles, short stories and ghost-writing a book. His preference is for writing short stories, with which he has had success in the women's magazine market and in competitions.

Renewed and Restored
Week 1: Friday

Jeremiah 33, verses 6 &7

'I want to tell you something,' he said. I wondered what was coming. I got ready to hear a tale of abuse or bullying or troubles at home, and steeled myself not to be shocked, but to listen and show no outward sign of emotion.

'I'm a Christian,' the fourteen-year-old blurted out, 'but I can't tell anyone. It's not cool. They'd tease me, make fun of me. You won't tell anyone, will you?'

Just one of the concerns – one of the lesser problems – faced by many of today's teenagers in an increasingly stressful world. A year or so ago, in the county where I live, a conference of school staff faced up to an epidemic of self-harm among schoolgirls, sharing their experiences of tackling the problem. A couple of the schools had turned to local churches and Rotary clubs.

'Can you help? Do you have people with life experience, good listeners who could spare some time to support youngsters with pastoral needs?'

The world's sin, not theirs, children caught up in domestic violence, pawns in battles between embittered parents, children who know no father or have two. Children whose parents don't care. Children whose parents were victims of dysfunctional families blighted by drugs or alcohol forty years ago. Children who have plenty of the world's goods but are poverty-stricken of parental time and love. Children who are different and become targets of scorn and bullying. Children who are overlooked. Children who are damaged and need rebuilding.

So many of these young people need confirmation that someone cares. They think their problems are their fault, they are to blame. Their self-worth, their value, needs to be restored and recognised. *As they were at first...* quotes the Bible text, but was there a 'right state' or had many of these children no proper starting place?

All children, all human beings have potential. That potential needs to be rebuilt and restored, options for the future widened. God's love for each child needs expression. Research into the lives of over a hundred children found living on the streets of our own country found that if there was just one adult that the child could trust, who cared and quietly supported, then the chances of rehabilitation of that child were significantly enhanced.

The Challenge

Could you be that adult? Is God calling you to reflect his love for such children? Most secondary schools have access to professional counsellors for the most disturbed children, but with local authority cutbacks on youth services, young people's mental health services and school funding, the opportunity to mentor a child or children through the schools may exist in your area. Usually secondary schools have the biggest needs but I know of churches that mentor the older children in primary schools. You need of course to be DBS checked, trained in safeguarding good practice, a good listener, patient and trustworthy of a young person's confidences.

DAVID MAIDMENT

Founder and past Chair of the Railway Children charity and retired Chair of the Children's Human Rights Network of Amnesty International UK. Brian now coo-ordinates a Street Pastor scheme (part of Ascension Trust), is a volunteer church children and youth leader and a mentor at two secondary schools. He is author of three historical novels (The Madonna Trilogy) which look at international social issues through the prism of traditional bible narratives, as well as having written non-fiction books on street children and railways.

Renewed and Restored
Week 1: Saturday

Psalm 51:10-12

Ruth started to unpack the box of odds and ends that she had claimed before the sale of her mother's estate. Her brother, Ron, had left it with her that morning. Before going on his way, he had slipped a piece of paper into her hand.

'Melissa's phone number. She would love to hear from you.'

Well, that wasn't going to happen, was it? She threw the note in the recycling bin.

Among the vases and brass bits and pieces, she pulled out the carving of a man's head. Ron's craft work from school. About fifteen centimetres in height, eyes asymmetric, nose prominent and arched, she could see why Ron found it an embarrassment.

Ruth caressed the wood, dust ingrained, a chip to one ear, the nose beginning to split, testament to years of standing proudly on Mother's mantelshelf. A quick dust was not going to be enough.

She scrubbed into the cracks and grain of the wood and washed behind his ears. With glue she mended the split on the nose, pleased at how much better it looked already. She placed it on the table to dry.

It was the nose that made her think of Melissa, at some family gathering when they were still school girls. Great Uncle Arthur – long gone, bless him – had admired the carving, and being short sighted, had held it close to his own face. It was a mirror image. Uncle Arthur had a huge nose too, and she and Melissa trapped hysterical giggles.

And then Melissa, always full of mischief, had the temerity to say, 'I like his nose.'

'Very handsome.' Uncle Arthur was always so kind and polite.

They tried to hide, doubled-over and helpless with suppressed giggles, like a pressure cooker, little squeals escaping from them.

So, it was sad they no longer spoke, and she avoided Melissa at any family gathering. The rift had happened when Melissa had gone behind Ruth's back and applied successfully for a job that she knew Ruth wanted desperately. Melissa had apologised but Ruth couldn't forgive her. All those years ago and it still hurt, even though her life had moved forward very well in another direction.

She thought she'd made a new start after her elderly parents had passed away. She'd taken out a subscription to a gym, stuck a diet plan on the fridge door, enrolled in a philosophy course, as well as taking on some secretarial work for her church. But something still didn't feel quite right.

The carving now dry, she polished the wood until it shone like new. What had she done with that telephone number? She retrieved it from the bin. Still she hesitated, added the number in her address book, bulging with bits of paper, and full of crossings out. She needed to sort out her contacts and buy a new book.

'Melissa would love to hear from you,' Ron had said. She knew what she must do.

'Hello? Melissa? Your cousin Ruth here,' she said into the telephone. 'I thought of you when cleaning up that school work of Ron's. The carved head. Do you remember how it resembled great Uncle Arthur?'

'Oh. The nose? When we were hysterical with laughter? So naughty.'

Ruth heard that old familiar giggle down the line.

Later she set the carved ornament on her mantelpiece where it settled humorously with her jade. She felt the joy of restoring her friendship with her cousin and of casting off the old bitterness at last.

Prayer

Father God, you know where we fail, where things get in the way of making our lives new and fresh. Search out the dusty crevices in our soul and make us responsive to your prompts.

Restore us and lead us to a purity of spirit that our joy may be renewed every day. Thank you for your lasting presence. Amen

EDNA HUTCHINGS
Edna lives in the beautiful county of Dorset and is a retired accounts assistant. She is a member of a United Church (Methodist and United Reformed). As well as writing, her hobbies include reading, knitting, walking and messing about with paints.

Renewed and Restored
Week 1: Sunday

Joel 2:25

I became a Christian when I was sixteen. I met Jesus and I set off after Him with determination and enthusiasm. Back then things were simple; I had most of the answers, if not all of them. I was ready to do what it took to follow him no matter what or where or when or how.

After a few years, my energy was diminishing. I followed, but a bit more slowly, with frequent rests. As time went on I followed the directions less and less, and took some lengthy diversions. Eventually, I lost sight of Him completely and went off on my own.

Those were my wilderness years. It's not an exciting story of being lost and dramatically found, just of gradually forgetting who I belonged to; a slow, imperceptible slide into half-heartedness and apathy.

One day, in a particularly miserable season of my life, an exhausted new mum, freshly bereaved and overwhelmed, Jesus came to find me again in my loneliness and grief. He gently reminded me of that summer day when I was a teenager, when He first introduced Himself.

Where Jesus is there is light and colour. I realised how faded my life had become.

Spiritually, these were lost years. I wish I hadn't wasted them. I wish I'd spent that time getting to know Him, hanging on His every word. I wish I'd consulted Him about key decisions in my life instead of believing that I knew best. I wasted time on things that were a poor fit; on relationships destined to go nowhere, on things that were unwise and sometimes damaging. I wish I'd invited Him into situations that affected me deeply – I suspect that some of those deep wounds and tender scars might have been avoided.

I could have been so much further down the road to spiritual maturity. I could have been wiser, more discerning; could have understood and developed my spiritual gifts, and helped people. I missed blessing after blessing because I was looking the other way. I didn't grasp wonders and mysteries that He offered me because my hands were full of other things.

Some of the saddest words in the world are *'It's too late'*. In those words lies an ocean of grief, hopelessness, despair, all kinds of loss. What might have been? Standing on the platform having run for the train, watching it leave without you, those dreams and hopes seem far out of reach.

I felt that it was too late. I was middle-aged; invisible and irrelevant. Whatever I might have done with my spiritual life, I'd had my chance and let it slip through my fingers.

And then I learned that this is not how God sees it. He says that it is *not* too late.

Not too late for a fresh start, to try again.

The Israelites, in the time of Joel the prophet, had wandered far from God, and not for the first time. Repeatedly He had warned them of the dangers of going their own way, of the consequences of not listening to Him. Disaster now fell on them, and it was devastating.

Their great city, Jerusalem, lay in ruins, their armies defeated and their reputation in tatters. Swarms of locusts devoured their crops, leaving nothing; green and fertile land left completely barren. All they had was taken from them, and the people were in despair.

But God had not forgotten them, and He had not stopped loving them. Even as they experienced the deserved consequences of their choices, He was with them in their distress, saying, *'It doesn't have to be like this.'*

It's not too late.

If His people were ready to come back to Him, He would not turn them away. He is the God of mercy – not only did He offer them reconciliation, but the promise of something more.

'I will restore to you the years that the swarming locusts have eaten.'

God told his beloved people that He would make it up to them. Israel's fields would be green again. Even after utter destruction, there would be a harvest. Not only is our God in the business of forgiveness, He offers restoration.

It's not too late.

What have the locusts taken from you? Maybe you took a wrong turn and believed that there's no way back. Something stopped you from reaching your potential and it's left you sad and resentful. Perhaps your dreams slowly died when things did not work out as you hoped.

Maybe your mistakes and poor decisions have led to missed opportunities and you keep wondering regretfully about the road not travelled?

That voice in your head – you know, the one that tells you that it's too late – that voice is lying to you. The voice that whispers that you're too old, not good enough, damaged beyond repair, that you're no use to Him; that you're defined by your mistakes and compromised by your misjudgements – that is not God's voice. The God who made you and calls you precious; the God who is the same yesterday, today and forever – He is saying to you:

'Come to me. I will make it up to you.'

Even as the Israelites lamented the devastation of their land, God held out His hand and offered them not only forgiveness, but reconciliation; not only reconciliation, but restoration.

You are loved, you know. Yes, even you. Just as you are – but God doesn't want to leave you like that.

He wants you to be all that He made you to be. He wants to pull you into His arms and meet your deepest need, whatever that need might be. Trust Him; He knows what it is.

He wants to heal your wounds, even the self-inflicted ones. He wants to give you back what has been taken from you and make you whole again. To bring fresh new shoots in the barren places – new growth where everything was dead.

New hope, where hope was gone.

It's not too late.

HELEN MURRAY
Helen lives in Derbyshire, England and has a blog, *Are We Nearly There Yet?* where she writes about life and faith. (www.hmarewenearlythereyet.blogspot.co.uk)

Renewed and Restored
Week 1: Monday

Job 42:10-11

Job—The Aftermath

Those would-be friends
Peddling folk wisdom, glib advice,
Not believing what you knew,
Your being right.

Well-meaning turners of the screw
With tables turned,
Once preaching through your abject need
Then made aware,
A costly lesson learned,
That they were hanging on your prayer.

Did you feel smug? Surely not you,
By then hammered like a sword,
Your pride's impurity, heat-wrought through
And out your pores
On the anvil of the Lord.

All that then life and more restored.

I scarcely dare to ask
Was it worth it—all the loss?
The question seeming crass,

For what could ever meet such cost?

But you who never found out why,
Saw God,
And thus, despised yourself

And then in Him were satisfied.

IAN MANIFOLD

Ian is a retired cancer specialist and currently Chairman of CVM, Christian Vision for Men, (www.CVM.org.uk). He has contributed several chapters in books for CVM including in 'The Code' and 'Founding Fathers'. He blogs on the CVM blog, mainly with poetry, often under the heading 'Code Odes'.

Renewed and Restored
Week 1: Tuesday

Zechariah 9:12

Hope can be a painful thing. Beautiful, yes. Powerful, yes. By its nature it is reality-defying – it is based on the still-not-yet of life.

We might think, sometimes, that it would be easier *not* to hope, instead to settle for our current realities and 'just get on with it', without this yearning within us. Within hope there can be discontent – we are aware of *what is not yet true*. This can hurt.

When we have faced ruin and exile, as ancient Israel did, hope may feel too much to bear. We're worn out, ground down. As another writer put it, 'Hope deferred makes the heart sick' (Proverbs 13:12).

And yet, even if we weary of it, hope can snag us still – whether we want it to or not.

When I am consumed with doubt or cynicism – as I too often am – hope still sticks, stubborn, in one small part of my soul. It is that which keeps me from giving in to the emptiness. The suspicion that, despite that incoherent muddle of my heart – *it might yet be true*.

The Holy Spirit sidesteps my darkness and nudges at that point of light.

I am pulled back, again, to the belief which has shaped my life. Back to the stronghold.

This evocative verse in Zechariah chapter 9 is part of a well-known passage declaring the future return of a King – *the* King, 'humble and mounted on a donkey' (v.9). Because of the 'blood of my covenant with you', God says, the prisoners will be set free from 'the waterless pit' (v.11). Here is a promise; here is a future. They are freed from the pit, but hope holds them still. The 'prisoners of hope' are called to return to their stronghold – the fortified place, the place of protection, to await full restoration. (The word translated as 'stronghold' here is not used anywhere else – it may refer to Jerusalem, their place of waiting.)

Stronghold, fortress, rock – elsewhere biblical praise-givers use similar terms for God; when I read 'stronghold', that is what comes to mind, that is how my heart responds.

In the stronghold, I wait for promised restoration.

In the stronghold I stand, a prisoner of hope.

Where Israel was assailed from without I am frequently assailed from within: exhausted, thirsty for God and yet drinking at all the wrong waterholes.

What we feed grows.

What we water flourishes.

What have I fed and watered in my life? And what have I allowed to become weak and dry? How many times have I wandered away from the One who sustains me and gives me strength?

To be restored requires a kind of journey, a reawakening. It may be long-anticipated, yet at the same time unexpected. Our hopes of being restored may grow weak.

Hope is not an easy thing. Sometimes it is just one long, thin thread connecting me still to the truth I profess, when I would rather give in and cover my face.

And yet, for all its chafing, my greatest fear is that one day that thread will snap. That hope will cease.

I scurry back to the stronghold, begging, do not let me go; do not release me from hope. Keep me, God, keep me.

I lift up my eyes
longing for restoration
as they did in days of old.

My hope is theirs; my king is theirs,
he rides into my life.

He tugs at the threads of hope
and I see, at last,
that they are not a tangled mess,
as I thought,
but an intricate, woven pattern,
multi-hued, tinted with forgiveness,
with grace.

How does the term 'prisoners of hope' make you feel?

Where, in your own life, are you longing for restoration?

How might the season of Lent lead us to a place where we can be restored?

LUCY MILLS

Lucy Mills is the author of *Forgetful Heart: Remembering God in a Distracted World* (2014) and *Undivided Heart: Finding Meaning and Motivation in Christ* (2017), both published by Darton, Longman and Todd. She also writes feature articles, poems, prayers and other worship resources.

www.lucy-mills.com

Week 2:
New Covenant, New Heart

Introduction
Dan Cooke

Before Jesus stepped into the lives of those he saved, including us to this day, we were ultimately the by-product of the world we lived in, the world that mankind helped to create. The problem was, as broken people in a broken world, we couldn't see the damage. It was as if we were looking at the world through a cracked pane of glass, but with no perception of the clarity of the real world. We assumed it was natural for everything to be unclear and have undefined lines running through them.

The change that overcomes us when we accept God into our lives allows us to not only see that the cracks are there, but that we can't fix the glass. Instead he moves us to another window, one with a perfect, unbroken view of him. Our focus has changed.

Dan is the Technical Support member of the ACW Committee. He is also a creator of characters and premises, with 140 different Characters, 9 species of Dragon and 9 A.I.to his name, all without ever actually finishing a single project! The master of the Starting-a-project-but-never-finishing-it, he hopes to get past this one day and put all his creations to good use.

New Covenant, New Heart
Week 2: Wednesday

Jeremiah 31:33-34

How did people in the ancient world connect and form relationships? Kings, nations and individuals made treaties and alliances: *covenants*. To make a covenant was literally to 'cut a covenant' and something had to be cut apart which could not be uncut. The blood of a sacrificed animal or bird symbolised something utter and pure. Blood meant life, and could bind together unrelated families or people of unequal status to form a new bond.

Perhaps the sight of death demanded that the parties take the bond seriously. Covenants were serious stuff. They frequently came with promises of blessing, if kept, or curses if rejected by one of the parties. Ancient peoples living near the Israelites made formulaic covenants which looked similar to ones we see in the Old Testament; God spoke in a way his people would understand. Guarantee. Pledge. Promise. Purity.

I took my son

God initiates covenants to form relationships with people. He made a special covenant promise to Abraham in Genesis 15, telling him to walk a path through animals which had been cut in half. He promised an exciting but seemingly unlikely future of a land full of his own descendants, and Abraham trusted him. God then told him to have his sons circumcised; another cutting to serve as a symbolic reminder of the relationship between God and his people.

And when the week was done

There was an even more important covenant that God made at Sinai in Exodus 19-24. Through his envoy Moses, God entered a special commitment *to* and *with* the house of Abraham. God promised to bring them to the land and to bless them, but the nation had to pledge to be distinct and different from the other nations around them. Their holy God demanded adherence to laws of holiness to set them apart. Laws inscribed on great stones. As a symbolic reminder, there would be a Sabbath rhythm to life, so that rest and work each had their place.

Gave thanks

The Israelites did not intend to displease God and break the terms of the covenant he had invited them into; a covenant they had so willingly agreed to in the desert. But when they arrived in the land they got distracted. There were so many good things, so much demanding their attention, and worship, and blood. Generation after generation followed the wrong gods. Instead of thanking and praising their loving Father God, the Israelites stumbled off course, compromised and cut themselves off from holiness.

Time and again God reminded his people that he wanted them to return to him, to stop breaking his covenant.

And broke him

Jeremiah was frantic. He pleaded with the people and the leaders to listen. He prophesied warnings and tried all sorts to get attention, but it was already too late. The people had utterly, wilfully and unrepentantly broken the covenant. Only one thing remained for God to do in response.

But would he do it? Would God allow another empire from the north to consume what remained of his chosen nation? The kingdoms of Israel and Judah had been cut apart generations before and Israel had already been exiled for breaking God's covenant. Surely not Judah as well? Judah was where God's temple was and where everything that symbolised God's relationship with his people belonged.

God had to allow it. He had kept his side of the deal. The people had utterly broken their side. The binding curses of the covenant would be meted out: the land would be abandoned and given rest; the families dispersed; the promised protection removed.

This grieved God enormously, but his love was bigger. God was not content to leave the people he loved, so a bigger, deeper covenant was required—one which did not rely on people's adherence to laws, but where all their offences were paid in blood—*innocent, pure blood* powerful enough to bind across different families and status. God wanted mankind in his family. The only reason that makes any sense of this is his enormous love. He hints at it in Jeremiah 31. After those days, the days of exile, a new day will come, and with it a new and bigger covenant. Ultimately, not only for the house of Israel, although it speaks the cultural language of the ancient law. As God had told Abraham, 'all peoples on earth will be blessed through you.' So, instead of legal requirements, *grace*.

'Listen,' God says to Jeremiah, 'instead of stones, I'll write my law on your hearts.' In this context 'hearts' doesn't mean our emotions, but our thoughts. Our thinking and reasoning influence our outer life; God will inhabit our decision-making and wills. We will want to live in ways which please him.

'I'll be your God,' he continues; 'you'll be my people'. Just as he always has, God still desires close relationship with people.

'You'll know me,' he smiles at his weeping prophet, '*all* of you.' The character of God's people will change as we know him both personally and together. Society will look different as our hearts start looking like his: ethical and social justice will demonstrate what God's love looks like and how it can touch anyone and everyone.

'And I will *forget* your sin,' he says, knowing that even Jeremiah wouldn't understand what that had to mean. God will choose not to remember our guilt. He alone can forgive us and transform us right the way through, because he alone is able to seal the covenant and pay the blood sacrifice.

Further reading

Hebrews 8-10

Prayer

Thank you, O God, that you forget my sin.

I cut myself from you, chose death.

You took your son, gave thanks and broke him.

Cut through me with your covenant of love.

It bound me. Though I strayed, you found me.

You cleansed me Lord;

Now let my heart and thoughts beat time with yours.

I want to be in covenant with you.

LUCY MARFLEET

Lucy blogs at www.lucymarfleet.com and has a passion for the Old Testament and for God's grace working in ordinary lives. Her children Lily and Joe keep her grounded and her husband Matthew lets her write, for which she is incredibly grateful.

New Covenant, New Heart
Week 2: Thursday

Isaiah 54:10

'My world has fallen apart' is a cry we sometimes hear when disaster or tragedy has struck. Family bereavement, accident, serious illness, redundancy, war or broken relationships can be just some of things that turn life upside down.

When I received the remit for this chapter, my mind and computer screen were blank. My husband had just been taken to hospital and lay seriously ill. A biopsy had led to the complication of sepsis. No-one seemed to have the time or inclination to tell me what was going on, but my suspicions were confirmed when a nurse said, 'You do know that sepsis can kill?'

Amazingly, there was peace. It was the kind of peace that you float along on, and as the days progressed, the peace carried me. It has continued through his diagnosis of cancer, and the wait for news of further scans.

As I have been re-reading the book of Isaiah, I have imagined myself to be in the crowd listening to the prophet thundering out his message. I sense myself cringing as he delivers the edicts of judgement and the need for repentance. But something holds me to his words as he continues with comfort and hope, and some amazing prophecies about a coming Messiah.

I have tried to imagine what it was like to live in ancient Israel where life was lived by a code of laws. A law for this, a law for that... hundreds of them to be observed every day. Talk about a 'tick-box' life style. The daily routine of finding and fetching water, grinding corn and collecting fuel for a fire to cook on, makes me weary even to think about it, and that was before they even started on the laws. Would I, as a woman, even have been allowed to stand and listen to the prophet, I wonder.

The people had not yet experienced the new covenant. But here was Isaiah telling them about a *covenant of peace*. I wonder if they even understood what a covenant was. But it is the promise of peace which draws me back to these words time and time again.

I had read the gospels so many times but I will never forget the shock I felt when some words jumped out at me one day. 'While he was saying these things to them, behold, a ruler came in and knelt before him, saying, *'My daughter has just died, but come and lay your hand on her, and she will live.'* Some translations say 'knelt and *worshipped* him...' Worship? Would that have been my reaction? I suspect I might have come kicking and screaming.

I did a study once on different people in the Bible and how they responded to life-threatening situations. Time and time again I found God's people standing firm in worship when life seemed desperately unfair, but as they did so, God's power was released in remarkable and often unexpected ways.

Now, as my husband has been told the cancer has spread to his bones, we face an uncertain future. His rising blood test results had been missed and, as a result, he has serious complications which might have been avoided. How will we react?

As we watch the news from around the world of earthquakes, famine, ethnic cleansing and war, we thank God for the blessings which we have. For us the mountains have not departed as they have for some people and we are so grateful for our home comforts.

I remember Paul, in prison, writing to the Philippians, and reminding them not to fret or be anxious over anything. 'Nothing at all?' I hear myself mutter. 'But surely it would be acceptable to be anxious about this... or that...?' Paul continued to exhort his readers that their attitude should be one of thankfulness, reminding themselves constantly that the Lord is near. They could continue to bring their needs to God in prayer – there was no need to pretend or be in denial – but to do so in an attitude of gratefulness and trust. Then there came a wonderful promise, that there would be peace. It would be peace that outstripped any imagination or outward circumstance, and it would be a peace that would stand guard over them. Even as I read his book I have a sense of bubbling joy which would be ridiculous in the circumstances if it were not so amazing.

I used to think that 'surrender' was a sign of weakness, but now I see that it is place of safety. As I yield our situation with open hands to God, giving him the right to do whatever he knows best, then I find peace. With his hands underneath mine, I can release the issue and I no longer carry the intense weight of it.

The new covenant, much like a Will or Testament, would only come into force on the death of Jesus. But in that dreadful moment, when the veil of the temple was torn in two, the way was opened up for us to have access to the Father. We are no longer bound by myriad sets of laws but we are invited into close relationship with Almighty God. As Paul explains to the Ephesians, we can sit with him in heavenly places. Head knowledge can be a reality in our hearts and, just like sitting with a close friend, we can be totally real. Jesus himself said that he did not call us servants but had chosen us as his friends.

New covenant, new heart. As we receive this amazing gift of compassion and peace, may you, the reader also experience its reality in your own life and situation.

MARGARET GEE
You can find out more about Margaret at www.unfoldingpromises.com.

New Covenant, New Heart
Week 2: Friday

Galatians 2:20

I lie on the ground, dazed by my fall. Not sure how long I've been here. My armour, split on impact, reveals my soft silken shell and the cool autumnal air revives me. It felt so good high above the landscape, looking out on the beauty of the countryside, with my brothers and sisters around me.

Now I'm on the forest floor unsure about my fate but I've heard whispers on the wind. Will I be consumed as dinner by a ravenous hog or horse? Placed as an item of beauty on a shelf or sideboard to be admired and adored? Used as an item of war in children's games, brother against brother? Wondering if I'll be the long-standing victor of hundreds of battles or shattered by the first blow.

Or maybe, maybe my biggest fear awaits me. Being trodden into the ground, trampled on by a herd of deer or a family out on their Sunday stroll. Forgotten, unnoticed, unwanted even. Going deep into the dense dark earth, past earthworms, beetles and the roots of my ancient ancestor, until I stop. Then I'll have to wait, for how long I don't know. Days, weeks, months, years even. At the precise right moment though, a storm will pass. Life-giving water will trickle down to where I lie. Then the pain will begin and from the moment it starts I'll want it to be over. It will be so intense that I'll feel as though I am dying yet strangely I'll also be changing. The process will have begun and I'll be becoming something new, something I didn't expect or maybe even want to be. A tree.

Saying it aloud somehow takes some of the fear away as my future is all so unknown. I may grow to be a tall, solid specimen that lives for 300 years or I may not even survive as a sapling. My creator knows though and that gives me all the peace that I need.

MARTIN HORTON

Martin lives in Sheffield with his wife Eva and dog Charlie and is the editor of the prayer diary for Wycliffe Bible Translators. He's recently finished his first children's picture book *Buffaloes on the Bed* and is now working on the prequel.

New Covenant, New Heart
Week 2: Saturday

Hebrews 9:15

A lonely track up a Dartmoor tor, in a landscape wild with coconut-scented gorse and delicate bracken fronds. Ponies graze beside a pool, the breeze sifting their manes.

From a distance, she looks like a girl, keeping fit perhaps, her blue fleece unzipped, her stride determined, a small rucksack bouncing on her back. She is athletic, yes, and strong-minded. Indomitable in many ways. She speeds up, as if to prove these things. Stones skitter away from her feet; a sheep scuttles away in alarm.

Estrild is not a girl. She's a woman of forty-two, and she's desperate to be alone. The children are with Tom's mother. Estrild is running, following the narrow path, up and up, coarse grasses scratching her legs. She's sweating now, her pace more urgent. She scrambles up the tor, stumbling over a patch of rocks, grazing her knee. She barely notices the pain. She stands, panting, surveying the wilderness. This is where they stood together, their special place, so beautiful it spoke to her, to both of them, of something eternal.

There is no peace today. Nowhere will ever be peaceful again. Estrild covers her face with her hands, and howls. Then she gazes into the distance, where clouds paint the land with shadows and everywhere seems empty and threatening.

Estrild moves around the tor, finds the sheltered place Tom showed her. He used to come here with Maxine, he said, before… She'd seen their wedding photos hidden away in one of Tom's drawers. She wasn't jealous, not at all. Tom deserved a lovely wife like Maxine. Life was a pig sometimes, taking a young woman like Maxine in childbirth. Taking her own husband when their daughter was only two years old. They'd had their fair share of tragedy, he said. That was what brought them together.

At first it had been simple. They had much in common – they both liked jazz, running, quiet meals at home after the kids were asleep. To their friends, it seemed to be working so well. If only Estrild had followed the rules. If only she hadn't ruined their lives.

She has no choice. Tom will get over her. He got over Maxine, didn't he? Mostly anyway. By some miracle, he loves both the children equally. 'Why can't I?' she sobs. 'What's wrong with me?'

She opens her rucksack, takes out a package, holds it in her hand. She can't go on being this kind of person any longer. It's not fair to any of them. She holds her breath, opens the tissue paper slowly, and there it is, red for danger, the sharp cutting-knife with the retractable blade. They last used it when they wallpapered the living room, working till midnight while the children slept. The room looked beautiful now, full of light, a place for games and toys and laughter, Tom said. If only he knew.

If she does this now, he won't ever have to know, will he?

Estrild runs one finger along the knife. Perhaps her body will rot away before anyone finds her. Please don't let her daughter ever know the truth. She flicks the blade out, ready. Her ears are filled with a high-pitched whistling. Her hand shakes.

There's a noise, not the neigh of a Dartmoor pony, not the bleat of a sheep. A human voice. She sits as if frozen. Is she imagining it? Her name. Called into the wind. 'Estrild, where are you?' She is so far from God, even He could not find her here.

'Essie! Can you hear me?'

Then Tom's squatting beside her, taking the knife, holding her, moaning, 'Why, Essie, why? What have I done?'

And Estrild is weeping, saying, 'Nothing, it's not you, it's me, it's what I've done.'

Tom lurches backwards. 'You've been with someone else, slept with them?'

'Tom.' Estrild can barely speak.

He holds his head. 'When?'

Estrild shakes her head. 'I have never been unfaithful to you, Tom, but I have been unfaithful to God.' She closes her eyes. 'You will hate me for what I've done.'

'Tell me.' Tom's voice is remote.

How can she explain? How can she tell him about the times she has deliberately and wilfully hurt his son, little Freddie? She has smacked him, hard, for throwing food, for scribbling on the wall, for hitting her daughter. For a hundred other offences, misdemeanours, call them what you will. For laughing in her face. She doesn't love him, and she cannot believe she ever will. And of course, Tom hasn't noticed, because the boy is clever, and behaves well for his father. She wants to die. It is best if she dies.

Estrild sobs. As she tells him, he moves away from her. His face is grey. He is angry.

'God is disgusted with me,' she says.

Tom slumps on a rock. He weeps.

'Go home,' she whispers. 'Leave me with the knife.'

'Essie.' Tom's voice is shaky. She waits for everything she deserves. 'It's been difficult for you. I didn't realise. I can't leave you here to die.'

Estrild shivers. If there is a hell, this is it.

'You need help.' Tom's head is in his hands. 'I'll take you home, but only on my terms, my conditions.'

She cannot look at him.

'I'm trying to understand. You should have told me. No, don't interrupt. I want us to live each day in a relationship of total honesty. You don't have to like Freddie, but you do have to love him. We'll deal with him together. If necessary, you must see a doctor.'

'You really want this?'

Tom nods. 'Commitment. A promise from you to resist all the pressures that threaten to break our new relationship.'

Essie is red-eyed, her throat constricted with grief and sorrow, and a desperation to take this new chance. 'I promise,' she says.

Tom takes her hand, and they stand, looking out over the Dartmoor they both love, and Estrild knows that now, all things are possible.

VERONICA BRIGHT

A retired teacher, Veronica has won over forty prizes for her short fiction. Her work has appeared in anthologies, online, and in three collections of prize-winning stories. She runs the Plymouth Writers Group, and is the short story adviser for ACW. Find her monthly blog at www.veronicabright.co.uk.

New Covenant, New Heart
Week 2: Sunday

Matt 26:27, 28

I sweep aside the protective sheet and sneeze as years of collected dust swirl around me in the gloomy attic. Wheezing heavily, I gaze at the boxes and pieces of furniture that have lain hidden beneath the cloth for so long. Mum never could bear to throw things out. They hold too many precious memories, she always insisted. All very well, except that I'm now the one who has to clear her possessions before the house can go on the market. I push that thought aside. She wrapped her memories round herself like a soft, winter cloak, and who am I to begrudge her that comfort?

I push cardboard boxes aside and make a pathway to the furniture: an old rocking-chair, a wide chest of drawers, a low cupboard with baby decals decorating the white paint and a Victorian cradle. I bite my lip as I approach the cradle. I hadn't realised Mum had kept it all these years. As soon as she fell pregnant, my father went searching for the perfect bed for me. He had found the cradle at an antique fair, she said, and spent many hours restoring it. She was so proud of him and wanted me to feel his love for me, but even now there's a hardness in my stomach when I think of him. All I remember is that he left us.

Despite the dull illumination in the attic, I can see the poor condition of the bedding, still in place as though ready for its inhabitant. The white sheets are yellowed and filthy now, the pillow with its frilled case looking lumpy and battered, and the patchwork quilt fraying at the seams. I wonder why it has been stored with such neglect. Why hadn't Mum packed the bedding away safely? Why was this so carelessly stored when she had taken such care with everything else up here?

I suppose she kept the cradle for the day that I should produce offspring. We were both to be disappointed. I suppress the twinge of regret that always assails me when I think about that. The doctors had all warned me I was unlikely to conceive—a potential side-effect of chemotherapy—but it never really stops hurting.

I look closer at the bedding and am convinced I've never seen that quilt. I have a vague recollection of the cradle standing in my parents' room when I was quite small, before I had to spend so much time in hospital; and of course, there are photographs of me sleeping in it as a baby; but this quilt feels strangely unfamiliar. It's silly to suppose I would remember anything, let alone everything, from such a young age, but it nags at me anyway.

I set that mystery aside and move the cradle out of the way to reach the open box lying behind it. I drag it further into the subdued light. Lying at the top of the box is a blue baby blanket, with a teddy bear and 'Thomas' embroidered in one corner. Confused, I lift out the blanket and see tiny clothes underneath. They look as though they've never been worn. I dig deeper and find a large envelope. Inside is a newspaper cutting. I recognise the smiling face of my father in the photograph, and I stare in shock at the headline:

MAN KILLED IN CAR CRASH
SAVES DAUGHTER

The article accompanying the photo is short and to the point:

Last night at 7.23 pm David Wood, 33, of South Croydon, and his new-born son, Thomas, were seriously injured when a tanker lost control on the M23 and the car they were travelling in was crushed between the truck and the central barrier. The baby was rushed to hospital but died soon after. Mr Wood, who had to be cut from the vehicle, suffered extensive injuries. Late yesterday evening he was declared brain dead.

Mr Wood's daughter Meghan, four, has been receiving treatment for tumours of the liver. Chemotherapy has proved unsuccessful at halting the disease. She was placed on a waiting list for transplant several months ago but there was no compatible donor. Her father was found to be a perfect match. This morning she received half of his liver in lifesaving surgery. (The other half will go to another recipient on the waiting list.)

His wife Margaret, 28, was unavailable for comment.

I struggle to breathe. Why don't I remember this? Oh, I know all about the surgery, of course. But—a baby brother? My father's liver? The sheet of paper slips from my shaking hand. The darkness of the attic oppresses me. I pack the baby items and make my way downstairs, box carefully manoeuvred down the ladder.

In the living room, I set the box on the coffee table and stare at the photograph of my parents hanging on the wall. I've never really forgiven him for leaving us. But now … I feel as though everything I ever knew, everything I've built my life upon, has evaporated. With a deep breath, I turn to re-examine the contents of the box. I lay Thomas's delicate baby clothes and blanket on the sofa. Further down I recognise some of my own baby clothes. Nestled among the layers of pink is a silver cup. I look at the engraving:

God so loved the world

and especially

Meghan

A box deep inside me opens and I begin to cry. The darkness I've been carrying for thirty years dissipates as I realise my father never deserted me. He gave me life. Twice. I wipe the tears from my eyes and read the words again. And as the enormity of the message of the cup hits me, I realise God never deserted me either. He, too, has given me life.

ADRIANNE FITZPATRICK

Adrianne has around 25 years' experience in the publishing industry as a writer (for adults and children), editor, teacher (of writing and editing), photographer, book designer and bookseller. She has had numerous short stories and articles published; and her first novel was published in 2014. She is currently working on another novel.

New Covenant, New Heart
Week 2: Monday

Luke 1:68-75

The traffic was minimal and the houses Saturday-afternoon lethargic as I walked home. But on the topmost branches of a tree perched an itsy-bitsy bird singing a song so raucous and extrovert that the tree winced and looked embarrassed. Like someone who takes a garrulous, opinionated relative into a library and regrets it.

My, my. What a voice for a bird so minuscule that had it lain in the road and chirped, 'Come on, pusscats – free meal!' I suspect local moggies would have sneered and moved on.

'I'm creating this itsy-bitsy bird,' said God, as he put the world together.

'With an itsy-bitsy voice to match?' suggested the angel assisting with Avian Innovation.

'You've not been listening, have you?' said God. 'If you had, you'd expect the unexpected.'

The first chapter of Luke's Gospel, from which our extract is taken, concerns the births of John the Baptist and Jesus. In particular, it relates the parts played by Zechariah, Elizabeth and Mary. These three people are itsy-bitsy people, living unremarkable, itsy-bitsy lives. Not one would, had they lived today, even qualify as a B list celebrity, the type who gets invited onto *Celebrity*

Masterchef or *Strictly* and has a bemused nation Googling their names. Zechariah is only one of 18,000 priests in his division and it's by lottery that he is chosen to burn temple incense at all. He lives in the hill country with his wife Elizabeth. She is childless, something she herself calls a 'reproach'. Mary is a young girl, betrothed to a local carpenter. She, along with Zechariah and Elizabeth, are unexceptional. So far.

But God isn't interested in celebrity, popularity or notability when he looks for people to use. He doesn't care who's heard of us, or who hasn't. He doesn't select the select or favour the already-favoured.

Conversely, *his* person-specification lists faithfulness, humility and servanthood as desirable qualities. According to verse 6 of the chapter, Zechariah and Elizabeth, despite the disappointment of childlessness, 'were both righteous before God, walking blamelessly in all the commandments and statutes of the Lord'. It's interesting that Zechariah collects this 'walking blamelessly' credit. He's clearly blamed by a miffed Gabriel for expressing doubt when the angel tells Zechariah his aged wife is to have a baby. Did the old priest perhaps turn to a neighbour and comment that the angel should have gone to Specsavers? It's understandable.

Mary too shows puzzlement at the news that she has found favour with God and will bear a child. She is a virgin and a nobody: how can this be? But her quick submission to God's will tells us much about her lack of self-regard. The prophetic song she sings when visiting the pregnant Elizabeth expresses her amazement at being chosen. 'He has looked on the humble estate of his servant. For behold, from now on all generations will call me blessed.' What kind of God is this, who takes the rawest, humblest, least-regarded people and gives them huge voices and roles in his kingdom plans? Elizabeth feels similarly touched by the honour afforded her. 'And why is this granted to me that the mother of my Lord should come to me?'

This leads us to Zechariah's own outburst of prophetic praise, which occurs immediately his tongue is loosed from the temporary silencing Gabriel ordered. I love the gracious irony of this: God gives Zechariah a significant speech after months of silence, as though saying, 'Here's your voice back, Zechariah, with interest. Now sock it to them.'

Zechariah does not crawl in the dust of the temple, as I would have, groaning, 'You can't use me, God. I actually questioned the angel Gabriel. I'm such a muppet.' No. He speaks confidently, faithfully conveying God's message to the listeners.

It's the kind of humility God loves. It's neither self-abasement nor false modesty. It's honest and sincere servanthood.

Zechariah echoes the theme already established by the two women: God takes the humble and raises them up. The Lord God of Israel doesn't just visit his people, unfaithful and fickle as they are: he redeems them. He finds a way to save them so that they can be part of his family. He takes the flawed and troubled servant that was King David and chooses his family from which to raise up the one who brings salvation. He speaks through the 'holy prophets' including some who didn't exactly cover themselves in glory. He keeps his promises to the holy fathers even when those holy fathers threw them back in God's face. He saves us from our enemies and those who hate us, even though we don't deserve that mercy. And, finally, our destiny is to serve the living God without fear: a high calling, indeed.

That's some speech from a man who's spent months shamed into silence. No wonder his neighbours were surprised.

Zechariah reminds me of Susan Boyle. Watch again her first audition on *Britain's Got Talent* in 2009. As she stands on stage, socially naïve and nervous, stumbling over her words, there are sniggers and rolled eyes from the judges. The audience is restive. Surely public humiliation is imminent.

Then she delivers *I Dreamed a Dream* as though she's sung from the cradle. She is preternaturally talented and yet unselfconscious, ordinary and humble. She even walks from the stage afterwards without waiting for the accolades and has to be called back.

The presenter turns to the camera and says to us, 'Well, you weren't expecting *that*, were you?'

No, we weren't. But we should learn to, because granting loud, significant voices to itsy-bitsy people is something our new covenant God loves to do.

We don't have to wait for a big stage. We just have to wait, humbly, for his nod.

FRAN HILL

Fran is a freelance writer and English teacher based in Warwickshire. More information about Fran is available from her website www.franhill.co.uk as is her first book *'Being Miss'*. Her second book is currently on tour in search of a publisher.

New Covenant, New Heart
Week 2: Tuesday

Luke 2:29-32

I

A seed from somewhere:

thistledown laid by the breeze

a moment on you

II

There was an old Hebrew named Simeon

Who lived life as God's faithful minion;

He knew that the Lord

Would abide by His Word:

A matter of fact, not opinion.

III

At the end of the day, the words of release:

Now, go – you are dismissed. For you, bondsman,

all the work is done and the waiting: it began

with a promise, and now it is ended. Peace.

You can die. You can go to the shadows, sleep

beyond the temple's flickering light, as doves

go silent, sacrificed; as clouds lift above

the settling land, and the waves fold in their deep.

But how did you know Him? After all those years,

the answer was – a child? Something in the eyes?

His cry? Something electric hit you, told you why

this was it, the end of death, the death of tears;

at last – the arc of gold in the prospecting pan

recalling you to wealth and life, and Everyman.

GEOFF DANIEL

An English teacher for 37 years, Geoff has been involved in poetry for longer. He has published one collection, besides other poems, articles and Bible study notes. The ACW Poetry Advisor, he writes critiques of members' poems, and has run workshops and competitions. He lives in Scotland.

Week 3:
New Heaven, New Earth

Introduction
Dan Cooke

While not extensively covered other than the fact that it will happen, there will come a time for the Earth as we know it, and the Heaven as we don't know it, to be overcome and replaced entirely by new versions. We do not know what these will be like, all we can know is that these will be the perfect versions of their former selves. However, we do have a preview, when Jesus came to Earth and died in our place. A view of perfect love.

Our perception of a new Heaven would be difficult to establish, for when we picture Heaven in our mind's eye we will all see something slightly different, while the underlying tone for all of us would be the Perfection of Christ, and that being reflected in Heaven itself. So, the concept of a New Heaven, and what it might be, is far beyond us.

Dan is the Technical Support member of the ACW Committee. He is also a creator of characters and premises, with 140 different Characters, 9 species of Dragon and 9 A.I.to his name, all without ever actually finishing a single project! The master of the Starting-a-project-but-never-finishing-it, he hopes to get past this one day and put all his creations to good use.

New Heaven, New Earth
Week 3: Wednesday

Isaiah 65:17

I am grateful for the abundance of promises in the Bible. I am grateful for the way they snag my heart with hooks of hope, in times of deepest need. I am grateful for this one, which I read, as I sat beside my sister's bed, days before cancer took her life, at thirty-five. I am clinging to all it promises, more desperately than ever before.

For me, this verse and the words that follow it echo with hope, depicting what some might call 'the now and the not yet,' – the sense that, as Christians, we have access to all that Jesus came to give – even while we live in a world where the complete fullness of all he offers is still in the future. He saves from sin and gives access to the 'inner throne room' of his Father, now. He grows and changes us, shaping us to be more like him, healing hurts, changing hearts. But there is still a 'not yet' element – there is still pain, suffering, struggle and tears that will one day be wiped away – but not yet.

Many point to pain and suffering (and let me be clear: this hurts – a lot!) as evidence that God cannot be real and active in our world. Surely, the opposite must be true. As I read this verse (and the passage it is part of), my soul resonates with its words, yearns for what they promise. That ache, that longing, I am convinced, points to something bigger, something better, something unimaginable now.

It gives me strength for the current age in which I live, where I have to cry and limp and cope in a real, painful world. It promises me that God has given me all I need, through Jesus, to stand when I feel like collapsing, to keep trusting when all feels lost. It gives me the courage to press on and the assurance that, in a far-off future age and place, the searing pain will fade, a mere hiccup in history.

I love the continuation of this passage: 'Never again will there be in it an infant that lives but a few days or an old man who does not live out his years.' I have experienced both: a stillborn baby as well as my sister's painfully premature death. I have walked through wilderness lands, wrestled soul-searching questions and shed an incalculable number of tears – and yet held on to faith instead of walked away. Why? Because of the story told in this short, Old Testament verse.

Through Jesus, there is help in our brokenness, light to navigate our darkness. We stumble and trip through the tougher things we face, but we are not alone and without hope. And one day, when this verse is ultimately fulfilled, I will stand in a beautiful, pain-free place, holding my sister's hand on one side and my daughter's on the other, and grief and longing and loss will be replaced with rejoicing and wholeness forever.

I need that hope to light my path through the fog that obscures in the here and now. A 'one day' and a 'not yet' that are well worth waiting for.

GEORGIE TENNANT

Georgie is a secondary school English teacher in a Norfolk Comprehensive. She is married, with two sons, aged 9 and 6, who keep her exceptionally busy! She can be found musing about life on her blog, as well as appearing, monthly, on the ACW *More Than Writers* blog. She writes the 'Thought for the Week' for the local paper occasionally too!

www.somepoemsbygeorgie.blogspot.co.uk

New Heaven, New Earth
Week 3: Thursday

2 Peter 3:13

John Newton's hymn *Amazing Grace* is one of our best known and best loved hymns, telling the story of our salvation in powerful poetry. But there is one verse which is seldom sung, and which doesn't even appear in many hymn books. It starts 'The earth shall soon dissolve like snow, the sun forbear to shine'.

I wonder why we don't sing this anymore? Maybe it sounds too much as if we are hoping for a nuclear holocaust! But even though we don't sing it, many of us still believe it, as part of a salvation narrative which involves the return of Jesus to take us 'home', the destruction of creation and our transmission to Heaven 'bright shining as the sun' (John Newton again, in a verse which we always sing with great gusto). This narrative can be extracted from selected Bible verses – after all, Newton got his inspiration from the Bible!

The verse we don't sing is probably based on translations of 2 Peter 3:12 which say that the earth and all the works in it will be 'burned up'. And of course, if we pursue that thought to its logical conclusion, then we don't need to bother about the world we currently live in. Global warming, carbon footprints, pollution of the oceans, destruction of the rainforests: none of it matters because it's all going to be burned up one day anyway, so we can live our lives as we want regardless of the effects on the world, ok?

No, not ok! There is wonderful, breathtaking beauty throughout the world. From towering mountains to hidden coral reefs; from the grandeur of thousand year old sequoia trees to the intricate beauty of snowdrops appearing for a few weeks every year; from the thundering power of a great waterfall to the stillness of a secluded lake; an inexhaustible mix of colours and shapes and textures and smells and sounds.

Why would God create all of this, and create in us the ability to be awed by it, and then burn it all up? In fact, the witness of the Bible is that creation is essentially good; indeed, it reveals and reflects the glory of God himself (go and read Psalm 19 – doesn't it make you want to shout praises from a hilltop?) And although creation has been marred by evil at the hands of men and women, it will one day be redeemed, in the same way as we who have been marred by evil are redeemed. This is seen most clearly in Romans 8, which expressly links the redemption of our bodies with the redemption of the rest of creation.

Here are verses 20-22: 'For the creation was subjected to futility…in hope that the creation itself will be set free from its bondage to corruption and obtain the freedom of the glory of the children of God. For we know that the whole creation has been groaning together in the pains of childbirth until now.' Note that creation is hoping to be set free, not to be burned up: ask any prisoner, and they will tell you that the two are not the same!

So, what about 2 Peter 3:12? Well, many recent Bible translations, based on other manuscripts, refer to the earth and all its works being 'exposed' or 'disclosed' or 'found to deserve judgment'. So, if there is to be fire, it will not be like a forest fire, wiping out everything that has life, but like a refining fire, destroying impurities so that the brilliance of that which is good and pure can be seen. When Peter talks about 'new heavens and new earth', he is talking about the heavens and earth made new or renewed, not about God throwing them away and starting from scratch. Don't ask me exactly how that will work in practice, as I don't know. But I also don't know how God transformed Jesus' earthly body into his glorious resurrected body, and that doesn't stop me knowing that he did it. What is certain is that it will happen, because God has promised it.

And there is more! The new heavens and new earth are to be a place 'in which righteousness dwells.' Note that this doesn't say, as we might expect, 'in which the righteous dwell'. How can righteousness, an abstract concept, dwell anywhere? To understand this, we need to understand that righteousness generally refers to a relationship of right standing, one in which we might say that all is well or all is as it should be between the parties to the relationship.

Through Jesus' death and resurrection, we are in right standing with God; all is as it should be. In the new heavens and earth there will be a three-way relationship between God, us, and creation, and every part of that relationship will be in right standing: us and God, God and creation, creation and us. Which leads us to the most challenging part of this passage: we cannot simply sit back and wait for a day to come when God will make everything all right. Instead, we should do everything we can to live in right standing here and now.

We know that is true in relation to our personal lives, how we relate to God and to each other, but what about our relationship to creation? Far from not bothering about it, we should be at the forefront of efforts to preserve the goodness of creation. How we do that will vary from person to person and from place to place, but living our lives as we want regardless of the effect on the world is not an option. As we await the promised new creation, let us both appreciate the glory of our world and do all we can to preserve and enhance that glory. And what about re-drafting that verse of Amazing Grace – how about 'We long to see the world renewed, it will with glory shine'?

GRAEME SMITH

Graeme Smith is a circuit judge and the author of *Was the Tomb Empty: a lawyer weighs the evidence for the resurrection* (Lion Hudson Monarch 2014).

New Heaven, New Earth
Week 3: Friday

Hebrews 12: 18–24

The first thing that strikes me about this passage is the strong contrast between verses 18-21 and verses 22-24. The first part is full of terror and dire consequences alluding to the account in Deuteronomy of the giving of the law to Moses on Mount Sinai. It paints a picture of God that I imagine in black and white and gloomy greys, as being all powerful but unapproachable and feared so much that the people dare not look at him or listen to his voice.

Then in the second part the picture changes dramatically, as here we have the Christian view of a new covenant and new relationship with God. This picture in my mind is painted in full colour: the city of the Living God, complete with rejoicing angels and the righteous spirits who have gone before us, worshipping the God of justice, and Jesus himself who made this new covenant possible by his sacrifice for us on the cross. His shed blood opened up the way of reconciliation with God – in contrast to the blood of Abel that called for revenge.

So no longer do we live under the law of an unapproachable God. Instead, through Jesus, we have access to a living relationship with God who not only loves us but knows each one of us.

As I started writing this I had just finished helping to compile a spirituality booklet to accompany the new

Forth to Farne Pilgrim Way that runs from North Berwick in the Scottish Lothians to the Holy Island of Lindisfarne in Northumberland, so the subject of pilgrimage is much on my mind. This booklet is not just about walking the walk, but about thinking the thoughts that are provoked by the various poems and reflections about our own pilgrim journey through life.

I have also been re-reading a children's version of the John Bunyan classic tale 'A Pilgrim's Progress' (retold by Geraldine McCaughrean, illustrated by Jason Cockcroft and published by Hodder Children's Books). This book loses nothing of the original story but paints the graphic picture in much easier language of Christian's journey through to the City of Gold.

When times are tough and we find ourselves in 'the Great Bog' or the 'Slough of Despond' we can easily revert back to the Old Testament image of a stern, punishing God, or indeed at times even doubt his very existence. But by keeping trust and faith and following the pilgrim path we can begin to find our way through the troubled times into calmer waters.

We remember too that in the Lord's Prayer we pray 'Your Kingdom come on earth as it is in heaven.' So guided by the Holy Spirit as we travel our own pilgrim journey we must try to seek ways to bring this about, by following the example of Jesus' perfect life showing love and compassion to all we meet on the way, until we come finally to our journey's end and find everlasting joy and peace.

A Pilgrim's Reflection

We are called to follow
in the footsteps of the first disciples
in the footsteps of the early saints

We are called to follow
in the footsteps
of faithful ones today

Jesus calls us to follow
in his footsteps on our journey of life.

HEATHER JOHNSTON

Heather is retired and lives with her husband in Coldingham in the Scottish Borders where I she is Elder and Young People's Leader in Coldingham Priory. She enjoys walking, especially by the sea, reading and writing and has self-published two collections of poems and prayers.

New Heaven, New Earth
Week 3: Saturday

Joel 2:28–32

Mattaniah stood gazing at the horizon. The pale blue dawn sky, streaked with lemon, showed no smudges of dark clouds. Perhaps the worst was past and they would not return.

He walked slowly across to his fig tree. It was stripped bare. Not one leaf left to shade him from the midday sun. The insect army had come with a rustle of a thousand papery wings. The incessant grinding of their mechanical jaws had transformed the green land around Jerusalem into a desert.

Mattaniah reflected bitterly on their power. They arrived. They ate whatever they wanted. His own powerlessness irked him. He had not been able to save one stalk. Now he would reap dust and stones.

He sat down heavily on the old wooden bench under the skeleton of the fig tree. It seemed that Yahweh had turned His face away. Even though Mattaniah had served faithfully in the beautiful Temple built by Solomon, and had taught the Law of Moses to countless young boys in the little school in his village, Yahweh, his God, remained distant and silent.

Each year, on the Day of Atonement, he watched the sacrifices and smelt the acrid, sprinkled blood. He saw the High Priest disappear into the inner sanctuary and wondered: did Yahweh whisper to him? What did the glory look like?

He couldn't help but feel pity for the two goats. What had they done to deserve such punishment? Of course, it was an honour to bear the sins of the nation.

Mattaniah watched the scapegoat and imagined his own sins taken by the animal into the wilderness and cancelled forever. He pictured the goat meekly bearing the heavy burden, staggering across the desert sands, stumbling at rocks, bleating piteously, until it grew exhausted and lay down to die.

When he returned home at the end of the day, he knew his heart was unchanged. He had not heard Yahweh's voice once, nor seen even a glimpse of His glory. Each year his dissatisfaction grew. It gnawed steadily at his certainty and hope.

A voice called out, 'Good morning, Mattaniah.' Roused from his reverie, Mattaniah squinted into the light. Who could be up so early? Of course – Joel! The son of his old friend, Pethuel, and the most diligent pupil at his school. He sighed.

The tall young man with tousled curly hair walked eagerly towards the fig tree and sat down next to Mattaniah.

'I had another dream! God spoke to me!'

Mattaniah winced; what was it about this time, he wondered. More visions of an impossible future? More pipe dreams?

'Good morning, Joel'.

'I saw it again – the Spirit of God, poured out like liquid fire on crowds of people, flaming power igniting their hearts. There were people from all nations and women too and little children.'

In his excitement, Joel had jumped up and was windmilling with his arms as if to demonstrate a rushing wind.

'Be careful, my son. Guard your heart and your tongue.'

'But I can see it – I can feel it all the time – burning, burning with fierce determination. Yahweh has such a clever plan – and it's for everyone – the whole earth–'

'Whoa – hold your horses, Joel, stop right there. You will land yourself in a lot of trouble talking such nonsense. Remember all I have taught you. You know Yahweh's words to Moses – His covenant is only with us, the sons of Abraham.'

'Ah, but what did He promise to Abraham? – "through your seed all nations on earth will be blessed" – so it is for everyone.'

'That's not possible, my son. Can you imagine all the tribes of earth coming to sacrifice at the Temple? All trying to squeeze into Jerusalem on the Day of Atonement?'

'But they won't need to because Yahweh has a better plan, a greater sacrifice, so that everyone can be saved.'

'Enough! Something better than the Day of Atonement? That sounds like blasphemy, Joel!'

'No, no, Mattaniah, don't take offence – just listen – listen to God. He'll tell you the same thing.'

'My boy, we have all we need and more.' Mattaniah gestured towards Jerusalem, across the locust-ravaged land. 'We are His chosen people, we have the Temple and the Law. Do not make the mistake of seeking for anything else – that leads to idolatry.'

Joel scraped the dusty earth with his toe. He looked up at the devoured tree. 'Yahweh is gracious and merciful. His love for you and for me reaches to the heavens. There is always more, dear teacher. So much more.' He patted Mattaniah on the back in an affectionate and sympathetic gesture.

The old man shook his head as he watched his pupil leave. He could feel the growing heat of the sun and stood up to return to his house. As he turned to go, something caught his eye. The tiniest flash of colour, a small beam of light in the scarified tree. He looked closely at the lowest branch. From the dried grey bark, a tender shoot was breaking through; it shone a vivid green; it was fragile; it promised life. Mattaniah touched it with a trembling hand and, at last, a steady pulse of hope began to beat in his soul.

JANE HENDRA
Jane loves to read and to write stories; she has written Christian drama and resources for children's church and she teaches creative writing.

New Heaven, New Earth
Week 3: Sunday

Philippians 2:1-11

For the Joy that Awaited Him
Once, before time, before any need of form
Or measurement, or name,
(All being known in joyous love and oneness)
Dwelling in darkness, richer than the core of the sun,
More dazzling with radiance, brilliant
With the passionate mysteries dreamt in the mind of
God.
Life, brimming with abundance, far beyond
The unknown, waiting depths
Of seas or forests, still uncreated and unnamed.
A ceaseless celebration,
An endless delight of inexpressible glory,
A jubilation of angels.

Then (and who knows when?) the choice, the risk:
To make known, reveal, a form, a Being
Comprehensible to faith, with all its possibility
Of love and reciprocity.
And all its possibility of loss.

A Word spoken: a Word that upholds
Universes, dimensions of space,
Pathways of stars exceeding all imagination.
Then, the naming of an unfolding creation   .

Calling it into form and presence:
Time, space, substance, light.
Dark. Day. Stars, sun, moon, night.
Fern and tree, grass, flower, fruit.
And creatures of gait and flight and fluid motion.
Then, Man and Woman.

And all things subject now to time,
In the eternal watchfulness of the sustaining Word,
To choose again: to lay aside that form of God
(Ignored, rejected or at the best, faintly perceived and
barely understood)
And enter through the confining womb,
And narrow gate of birth, to show in human form
Through thirty years,
The true and loving, patient nature of Himself.

And in the last acts of love,
To hold and wash with tender carefulness
The hardened, grimed and weary feet of friends
(His own unwashed),
And tear the bread and offer wine
For their refreshment.
And hear, so soon, how their feet fled from Him,
As His captors trampled the quiet garden.
Then, (He who is Word and Life), kept
Silent in the face of lies,
And the unrelieved torment of sun-darkening death.

Therefore, this Man, this Prince of Life,
Is liberated from the rock-hewn cave of our mortality,
And raised to exaltation.
Therefore, His Name is given for all humanity:

A door set open to that glory
Exuberant in the heart of God before the world
Was dreamed of, or spoken into form and being.
Therefore, His unimaginable beauty
Fills the limitless and radiant heavens,
Caresses the earth with promise.
At His return,
The gladness of our healed humanity's worship
Will join the angels' jubilation
In a restored and reconciled creation.

JANET KILLEEN

After Janet retired from teaching, she began writing; and her spiritual journey is reflected in what she writes – a collection of Biblical short stories, *Recognition*, and a recently published novel, *After the Flood*, 2017. Janet seeks to grapple with the realities of faith in a perplexing and often disturbing world.

New Heaven, New Earth
Week 3: Monday

Revelation 21: 1-5

Walking is one of my joys. There are times when the beauty of God's creation stops me in my tracks. But other times, the troubles of life seem so many. The world is full of pain. There are tragedies on a global scale. A new heaven and a new earth would be welcome. What will it be like? I find it hard to picture.

But just now, there are challenges closer to home.

'I'm going to die, you know.'

Here it is. The conversation I've been waiting for, and dreading. Don't fudge it now, I tell myself.

'Yes, that's right, Mum. You are.'

'I'm a bit frightened.'

We are coming to the end of our bedtime routine. The slow and painfully laboured trip to the bathroom is over, Mum is snuggled under her duvet, her body curled up and her face tiny against the pillows.

We have sung songs and hymns, though neither of us has a good voice, and recited poems.

'Let's end with a prayer now,' I say, putting down the poetry book and picking up the Book of Common Prayer.

'Must we?' she says.

'Oh, I think so. I think we should end with God's word, don't you, rather than W.B.Yeats'.'

'Go on then,' she says reluctantly. Her relationship with God has, on her side, sometimes been a bit tetchy. She's had a lot to put up with.

I have tried reading verses from the Bible, but they make no sense to her anymore, except Psalm 23. I have tried extempore prayer but she doesn't like it; so, we open her prayer book, signed at the front in her childish handwriting, then later, proudly, with her married name.

We pray together, 'Almighty and most merciful Father; we have erred and strayed from thy ways like lost sheep. We have followed too much the devices and desires of our own hearts....'

The words, like those of the poems learnt at school, come from the depths of her memory, where now only the events of long ago remain.

And now, she speaks of her death.

I take a deep breath.

'You're right, death is scary. But you know Jesus said there is nothing to be afraid of. He promises he will never leave us and will be with us always. He says that in God's house there are many rooms and He has gone to prepare a place that will be just right for you.'

'Why can't I go there now? I'm very tired you know.'

'Well, maybe your special place in heaven is not quite ready. Perhaps He's still putting in the finishing touches, painting the door.'

'Oh.' She is thoughtful, then adds anxiously, 'but I shan't want to leave you.'

'I know. I will miss you too, Mum.' She has no idea how much.

'And I will be joining you before too long. And just think, you'll see Dad again.' Mum cared for him so faithfully through the many years of his illness. 'And your mother and father and your little sister. You won't ever have to be sad again. It will be such a party in heaven!'

I think of the tears she must have shed when her sister died, leaving Mum to recover from diphtheria, alone in the isolation hospital. Three years later her mother died. Such sadness and so many tears cried: too many for one young girl.

The verses in Hebrews that talk about the great cloud of witnesses waiting to cheer her on as she enters the stadium for the final lap come to mind and I carry on;

'And not only your family, but all those others who've gone before: there'll be Abraham and Moses….'

'Oh, I don't think I'd like to meet them,' she interrupts before I can reel off the whole list. She looks worried.

'Well, I'm sure you won't have to meet them if you don't want to.'

I'm winging it now. In fact, I don't know what it will be like. The descriptions of heaven and the end times are way beyond my understanding, let alone Mum's. But I know that if Jesus says it will be good, then it will be. No more sin and pain. We will be with God forever, known and loved as already we are, but also able to perfectly love Him.

The end for Mum, when it comes, is not traumatic. I am with her on her last day. I'm not doing very well with the personal care bit, but the nurses come in and gently wash her poor worn out body; it is like an anointing. A profound peace settles in the room; God is here, the division between earth and heaven grows thin. The day becomes one of vigil. My daughter and Mum's great-grandson arrive. He plays with his toys on the floor, just a normal day for him. Neighbours pop in and out. The afternoon slides into evening. Her breathing changes. A friend comes. We sit, either side of her bed, and chat about ordinary things. We pray. I stroke Mum's hand. The colour of her skin is changing; it won't be long.

There have been times over the last few years that have turned out to be false alarms. Emergency calls from the hospital summoning us to her bedside, only to be told by the nurse next morning, 'She's been eating breakfast and singing to us "The boys in the backroom!"' It's been a rollercoaster ride, this journey towards the end.

But now, today, it is different. Her long struggle is finally over. She has completed the race that was set before her. She did it with determination and vigour, with love and fun – despite the tragedies that came her way.

Her life is slipping away. What a privilege to be here with her today as she takes her leave.

Through my tears, I hear myself say,

'You can go, Mum. They're all waiting. Jesus is there, and all your family. They're saying,

"Here comes Molly!"'

JUDY RAYMONT

Judy was adopted as a baby and is married to Nick. They have two grown-up children and four grandsons. They live in Cambridge and worship at Holy Trinity Church. Judy is a retired infant teacher and recent writer.

Blogs: www.wordsindueseason.wordpress.com

www.cambridgelackademic.wordpress.com

www.judesthameswalk.wordpress.com

New Heaven, New Earth
Week 3: Tuesday

Revelation 22: 1-5

In September 2017 I was asked to be a guest on the first of a new fast-moving magazine-style Sunday afternoon show on local radio. There would be two broadcasters, a local artist and myself discussing a variety of topics, including faith.

The show was recorded just after Hurricane Harvey hit Texas and the Caribbean with devastating winds and flooding. Hurricanes Irma and Jose were predicted to hit the area the following week.

As part of our topical discussion, the interviewer turned to me and said, 'We're getting more natural disasters. Think of those awful floods in Houston. I can't think anyone today would put them down to the influence of a god, would you?'

Not an easy question to answer in thirty seconds, and I'm ashamed to say I fluffed it.

Since then I've been thinking about what I would say if asked the question again. After all, when disaster strikes, it's a struggle to understand why an all-powerful, all-knowing, loving God doesn't intervene. What can be said to those facing unimaginable suffering without sounding trite, unfeeling or judgemental?

Does it help to point out that natural disasters don't increase deaths? Everybody is going to die some day. I don't think so. It's the tragic and senseless way they die that causes so much grief.

Would it bring comfort to explain that human sin has ruptured the perfect world God created, unleashing death, disease, famine and disaster? This is true, but to point it out in the aftermath of a tragedy would be insensitive at best.

Suffering people need hope, not theological lectures. They want to know others understand what they're going through. They want to believe things will get better and that the adversity they're experiencing won't be the last word. They long for something good to be redeemed from the debris of their lives.

Revelation chapters 21 and 22 describe a time when the earth will no longer be buffeted by disaster. A new heaven and a new earth will replace the old heaven and the old earth, and the City of God – the New Jerusalem – will come down from heaven and be established on earth. It will be a city ruled by God and His Son, Jesus Christ. From their throne room, a river of life-giving water will flow, not a stream of sewage or pollution or disease. The trees will produce fruit, not famine; their leaves will bring healing to the nations instead of sickness and strife. It's a city which cannot be shaken, flooded, bombed or invaded. It will be the home of God and His children, who will reign with Him for eternity. The ancient curse of sin will be lifted from our planet and our lives. No more darkness, no more death. Just love and light, health and harmony, elation and praise.

The great redemptive arc of the Bible takes the reader from paradise to paradise via the valley of the shadow.

By the end of the Bible, the Garden of Eden has been transformed into the City of God. Victory has been snatched from the jaws of defeat. Creation is restored and, as with all great books, the end is better than the beginning.

But right now, we inhabit the middle of the story, the mess and dramas and loose ends. One day a tragedy, the next a comedy. For those who question the existence of an omniscient, omnipresent, good God in the face of disaster, the Easter story insists that He has not abandoned us. Walking through the ruins, Jesus entered our broken world to come alongside those who contributed to that very brokenness. He suffered religious persecution, political oppression, homelessness, captivity, false accusations, betrayal, torture and crucifixion. He died the death that should have been ours to give us the life that belongs to Him. It is in Jesus that we see most clearly the love of God.

We don't have to experience a hurricane to feel our world has been shaken. Health problems, financial pressures, job loss, relationship breakdown and bereavement are experiences most of us will face at some point in our lives. And when we're suffering it's only human to ask 'Why?' and to be angry with God. But the more we look to Jesus and read His Word, the more our circumstances shrink to their proper perspective.

God is sovereign. He can be trusted even when it seems He's not on our side. One day His sovereignty will be visible for all to see. In the meantime, He has not left us alone in our suffering. He draws close to the broken-hearted, always moving to turn evil into good. He longs to comfort us so we, in turn, can comfort others. For those of us who have gone down into the shadow before coming out into the light, how much more wonderful that light is after the experience of darkness.

The book of Revelation tells us God's kingdom is coming. How can we know this vision of the future is true, and not just pie in the sky when we die? From our own stories. We can taste these blessings now. If we love God and trust in His Son, our spiritual thirst is quenched. We receive inner healing, and unity with our brothers and sisters in Christ. A secure foundation, freedom from bondage and the knowledge of the Fatherhood of God are ours. The light of His presence will drench our worship. Eternity is planted in our hearts. The New Jerusalem becomes the glorious fulfilment of the blessings we receive today, both individually and in our churches.

Calamities are a wakeup call. They impel us to question the foundation of our lives. They are an opportunity to grieve with those who grieve and to do what we can to alleviate their suffering. But through them we must proclaim that death is not the final word.

Earthly life is short. Eternity is long. This world is not the end. It's just the beginning.

KATHRYN HITCHINS

Kathryn writes contemporary fiction from a faith perspective. *The Girl at the End of the Road* was published in March 2016 by Instant Apostle. *The Key of All Unknown* (finalist, Woman Alive Magazine's Readers' Choice Award 2017) followed in October. *The Gardener's Daughter* will be released in Spring 2018 (www.kahitchins.co.uk).

Week 4:
A New Kingdom

Introduction
Amy Robinson

From the moment that John the Baptist started shouting about the kingdom of heaven being at hand, the stage is set for us to learn more about this mysterious, exciting, new rule of a heavenly King. 'The kingdom of heaven is like this,' explains Jesus in many a parable, and we start to get an idea of the shape of it, of its topsy-turvy values, of the way things really are.

But is it now or later? Are we looking forward to it, or has it arrived with its King on earth? Jesus talks about the kingdom as a tiny thing like a seed or like yeast, secretly growing until it reaches the point where it takes over the whole world.

In this section, we sift through the images of nets and fish, wheat and weeds, seeds and yeast, in search of the tell-tale gleam of gold: the hidden treasure of a new way of life in God's kingdom.

Amy is a writer, performance storyteller and ventriloquist, and the children's worker in her benefice. She has written three books about puppetry and storytelling and co-founded the storytelling company Snail Tales. She is the publicity member of the ACW Committee.

A New Kingdom
Week 4: Wednesday

Matthew 13:44

I loved drawing treasure maps as a child. My desert island drawings were filled with bendy palm trees, triangle-mountains and dots for sandy beaches with an X to mark the buried treasure. I spent hours daydreaming over them. But I always had trouble conjuring excitement over a chest of mere gold coins and jewels. As a child it did not seem real and meant little. Looking back, I think I would have been far more excited over a stash of buried books!

In the one verse parable above, Jesus likened the kingdom of heaven to buried treasure.

What is the Kingdom of Heaven?

There is a lot in the New Testament about the kingdom of heaven or the kingdom of God. Much of Matthew 13 is taken up with Jesus painting word pictures of what this kingdom is like.

The kingdom of heaven was ushered in by Jesus. It is a sure thing. The enemy has tried to sabotage it, but God has a master plan which the enemy, try as he might, cannot jeopardise.

The kingdom of heaven started small like a tiny seed but is growing into a large tree. As a small amount of yeast permeates the whole loaf, so the kingdom of heaven affects everything with which it comes into contact. We see God's kingdom touching earth when broken people are loved and cared for as precious; when we see people miraculously healed or set free from life-controlling issues. When we witness these things, we get a foretaste of what life will one day be like when the kingdom of heaven has fully come.

God's kingdom is how things are meant to be: everything perfect, everyone whole, no more pain or hurting or tears. It was never God's desire for bad things to happen, for crime and selfishness and violence. His kingdom is of power, righteousness, peace, light and hope.

Earlier in Matthew's Gospel, in the Sermon on the Mount, Jesus urged His followers to seek first His kingdom. He discouraged them from worrying about money and possessions. It was not that He thought these things were not important, but He knew the Father is fully aware of our needs, and will provide. That is what the Father does. Everything good comes from Him. Our responsibility is to seek first the kingdom and trust God to meet our needs.

This may sound hard, even irresponsible. A few years ago, I had a busy week at work preparing to go away on holiday. There was a lot to do and I didn't have a second to spare. But then God's presence filled my study: it was an invitation to me to worship and soak in Him. I took whole hours out of my day simply to enjoy God. In between, I worked hard. Somehow everything got done in time – and without me stressing about it. For me that week, seeking first His kingdom meant laying work aside and worshipping.

What is the Treasure?

Jesus Himself is the treasure. He came to give us abundant life; life that swells within filling us to overflowing with peace and joy and hope.

As young children are excited over a treasure map, so God wants us to be like young children with Him, full of anticipation and expectation that He is worth pursing and will not disappoint.

King David wrote that in God's presence there is fullness of joy and at His right hand are pleasures for ever more. God is not a spoilsport, issuing a long and boring list of dos and don'ts to His followers.

No, He promises good and positive things: fullness of joy and pleasure, with Him as our treasure.

A couple of years ago I went away to Hunstanton in Norfolk with a good friend. We had a prayer retreat planned and were expectant of meeting with God. But when we arrived, we realised that God had pre-planned this time and it was He who was inviting us to be with Him.

It was a wonderful week where we enjoyed a foretaste of heaven. His presence was with us, at times almost overwhelming. One morning I woke up early to watch the sunrise. I sat in the kitchen with Jesus, sipping coffee, and gazing at the sky as it changed from pale gold to rosy pink before the blazing ball of glory appeared on the horizon, shooting forth its rays. For one brief and glorious second the veil was taken away and I knew who

I truly am: a daughter of the Most High, beloved of God. One day I will shine like the sun in my Father's kingdom.

Jesus said that our hearts lie where our treasure is. As we seek first God's kingdom – longing for His rule and reign in our lives and in our neighbourhoods – the things that are important to God become important to us. In seeking first His kingdom and submitting to Him, Jesus becomes our treasure. The more of self we put under His Lordship, the more capacity we have for enjoying Him.

Yes, there are times when this is hard, when doubts filter in and we wonder if it is all worth it. But if we make it all about Jesus, it is easier to push through the hard times. Remember Jesus said it was for joy that the man sold all he had to buy the field and gain the treasure. Sacrifice becomes less of a hardship when we are pursuing a Person who shares His abundant life with us.

Jesus Himself is our role model in this. God the Son 'emptied Himself', as Paul puts it in Philippians 2, willingly and joyfully giving up His privileges as God to become human. He experienced weakness, misunderstanding, rejection and a terrible miscarriage of justice that ended with His execution. Why? For the joy that was set before Him: the joy of becoming the Way for you and me to come into His Father's kingdom and enjoy Him forever.

MANDY BAKER JOHNSON

Mandy Baker Johnson is a private medical secretary and freelance writer. She enjoys blogging at www.mandybakerjohnson.com and has co-authored a short devotional book, Drawn from Words. She volunteers with a

Christian charity working with women in the sex industry, and is currently researching this area for her second book.

A New Kingdom
Week 4: Thursday

Matthew 13: 45, 46

In the 'Pearl of Great Price' parable Jesus claims that His kingdom is worth a lifelong search and the surrender of everything we possess. Why? What does the kingdom of heaven offer that can't be found elsewhere? I believe it provides grace for the present and sure hope for the future.

Membership of God's kingdom gives us grace for the present by meeting our deepest needs – for unconditional love and acceptance and a sense of identity and belonging. This Easter billions of people all over the world will celebrate a 2,000 year old event because only through Christ's death and resurrection can we be reconciled to our Creator. Once reconciled, we can live in the security of His embrace and experience His living presence beside and within us.

In Christ, we receive a new identity as children of God and we belong to a worldwide community described by Peter as 'a chosen race, a royal priesthood, a holy nation.'* Whatever our background, in Christ's kingdom we are all equal in status and value, because we are all sinners saved by grace,

> *There is neither Jew nor Greek,*
> *there is neither slave nor free,*
> *there is no male and female,*
> *for you are all one in Christ Jesus.*

Galatians 3: 28

As if this were not enough, God's kingdom offers sure hope for the future – the promise of eternal life. Increasingly society is adopting an outlook championed in Queen's song, 'Who wants to live forever?' The alluring lyrics urge us to discard the outdated 'myth' of eternal life and embrace the 'sweet moment' – the here and now. In His parables of the kingdom Jesus addresses Freddie Mercury's question: even if heaven exists, why would anyone want to go there?

Random ideas about heaven have taken root in public consciousness. They depict eternity as a never-ending harp ensemble in the sky, playing to an audience of one – an old man with a long white beard! No wonder people switch off! But the Bible speaks of 'a new heaven and a new earth' where God will restore life as it was intended – with fulfilling, purposeful work, enjoyable leisure and life-giving relationships with God and one another.

The Bible excels at understatement and my favourite one is Revelation 22: 3, 'No longer will there be anything accursed.' This suggests we can begin to picture heaven by envisaging life with everything bad removed. In this scenario, what would we no longer need? Armed forces (no conflict), medical treatment (no illness or ageing), undertakers (no death), police (no crime), politicians (God will reign). Is it beginning to appeal?

Let's take a more positive angle. Can you imagine your 'bucket list' if time and money were not an issue? Now expand your vision – what would you like to do if you had *more than* all the time and resources in the world? My heavenly bucket list includes lots of travelling, learning to dance and sculpt, meeting some of my heroes like William Wilberforce and spending quality time with friends and family, not to mention a humungous reading list. Do I detect alarm bells? Sculpture, books – in heaven? A much overlooked passage about heaven is Revelation 21: 24, 26, 'the kings of the earth will bring their glory into it ... They will bring into it the glory and the honour of the nations.' Surely heaven will purify and glorify humanity's highest achievements, not obliterate them. Imagine all mankind's potential for creativity, innovation and technical ingenuity devoted entirely to good use – unlimited opportunity and endless possibility.

What no eye has seen, nor ear heard,

nor the heart of man imagined

what God has prepared for those who love him.

1 Corinthians 2: 9

Truly the kingdom of heaven is a pearl of great price, but who will pay? I believe Jesus chose the pearl because it's the only precious gem formed by a living creature and procured at the expense of a death. When a grain of sand gets stuck between an oyster and its shell, the oyster secretes layers of nacre. This shiny substance coats the grain of sand and, over the years, forms a lustrous pearl. But to harvest the pearl, the oyster must die.

To pay the great price for us, Jesus lived a perfect life and died a sacrificial death. For us, entry into the kingdom costs nothing but changes everything. It is not a democracy but a realm, ruled by a Sovereign – God. The merchant sold everything he had to own the pearl. Belonging to the kingdom demands that we abdicate from the throne of our lives and submit to Christ as Lord. This is not a single act but a lifelong process. The thought of relinquishing control is deeply troubling unless we focus on the Person to whom we surrender it – the Good Shepherd who lays down His life for the sheep. At the cross God proved once and for all that He is for us; we can surrender our autonomy to Him without a qualm.

This Lent, where are you on your journey of faith? Are you searching for the kingdom and not yet finding it? Persevere because God has promised to be found by all true seekers, 'You will seek me and find me, when you seek me with all your heart.'** Or perhaps like me, you're a weary pilgrim finding the cost of the Christian life high. Keep going, for by following Jesus, ultimately we cannot lose but only gain.

We possess the pearl of great price – a kingdom that is flawless, beautiful and everlasting. Let's rejoice in belonging to the kingdom of heaven and flaunt our jewel for others to see and desire for themselves.

'In [Christ] there dwells a treasure all divine,

And matchless grace has made that treasure mine.'

William Gadsby
(Immortal Honours rest on Jesus' Head)

* 1 Peter 2: 9

**Jeremiah 29: 13

MELANIE HODGES

Melanie writes Christian ethos children's fiction with strong traditional family values and Devotions for Christians living with chronic illness. Her titles, *Sirenna's Song*, *Sirenna's Secret* and *Patience for Patients* are available from lulu.com or by contacting the author at mel21hodges @gmail.com.

A New Kingdom
Week 4: Friday

Matthew 13.52

Twenty-one years ago, The Treasure Act was introduced in Britain. From that date onwards treasure that individuals found had to be shared with the nation.

Jesus would approve.

At the end of his parabolic teaching on the nature and value of the Kingdom of heaven Jesus asks a question. 'Have you understood all these things?'

'Yes' they reply, which leads on to today's reading and the phrase 'therefore' and when we look to see what it is 'there for' we find treasure, treasure that is to be shared.

Jesus describes old and new treasure brought out from a strong-room. The old is the wisdom of the centuries, the stories of hope and of Israel. The new is the Gospel, a new exodus from the slavery of sin and death, a pilgrimage to the promised land of the new Kingdom where God once again takes his rightful place amongst his people.

The possessor of the treasure is a scribe, one who knows his bible and sees in the ancient stories a new reality, for this person has been trained for the kingdom. Gone is the hoped-for 'last day' when freedom is finally found through God's military messiah; the last day has become 'today'. Hidden in plain sight, *God is now here*, gone is the despair that *God is no where*. This is treasure indeed to be brought out and shared. From the very beginning of life, to the beginning of every life, God is present, a golden thread of mercy and loving kindness running through human history, waiting to be discovered.

Jesus says the consequence of rightly understanding the teaching of the Kingdom parables brings a responsibility. The discerning scribe is described as the master of a house (*oikodespotes*). Such a person is one who distributes his wealth, either as wages for workers, as in the story of the labourers in the vineyard (Matthew 20.1-16) or rental property for farmers (Matthew 21.33-43). The expectation is that the priceless treasures of the kingdom are to be shared by those 'trained for the kingdom.' And that includes us, 'every scribe', as Jesus says.

God is now here is treasure, to be shared amongst those without hope in the future, who are enthralled by the past and seeking to escape the struggles of the present. The scribe trained for the Kingdom knows there is freedom from the ties that bind for s/he sees things differently. S/he knows where to create space so that God can be discerned in the here and now stuff of life, and such discovery offers life in all its fullness.

How do we bring out the treasure that lies within?

Here the parables of the Kingdom will speak to us.

We are all most likely a mixture of soils, selective in the reception of Kingdom life. What lies within may be arid, shallow or choked and we must look to see where the fruit of the Spirit is withered and address the reasons why it is so.

The Kingdom is contagious it spreads like the mustard seed and works silently like the leaven. Do we see that in others, in ourselves? This last year have we grown closer to God or further from him?

Most of all we must examine our priorities; have we discovered the incomparable value of the Kingdom? Will we give all to attain it?

We might ponder the fact that it is that which we treasure we are called to share. If we don't treasure the Kingdom we can't share the Kingdom, for we can't bring out what isn't within us. Perhaps we need to learn like Mary to treasure up all these things that are spoken about Jesus, the one to be called 'God with us,' and ponder them in our hearts (Luke 2.19).

Finally, Jesus says discovering the presence of Immanuel in our midst is an urgent affair, for the final Kingdom parable speaks of a separation of good fish from bad, of wicked from those declared righteous by God. It is a hard thing to hear and understand that Jesus, the most gentle and loving person, speaks with passion and urgency about impending judgement and destruction, of weeping and gnashing of teeth. A time will come, he says, when *God is no where*, and that will be a terrible thing. Until then we work with God who is in heaven and in our hearts, to share the news of this precious treasure, motivated by love rather than compelled by a law, living in the reality that God is now here.

Prayer

Lord, reveal your treasure that lies within us today.

Create in us a desire to bring out your precious gifts

to share with those in need.

Lord reveal the areas of our lives that are barren,

shallow or choked and bring your healing touch.

Stir a passion within us that earnestly seeks for your Kingdom to come yet more evidently in our own lives and in the lives of those who do not yet know you.

We make this prayer in the name and for the glory of the coming King Jesus

Amen.

REV NICK HARRIS

Nick is currently working to bring his debut novel *Nephilim Rising* to publication. This book draws on first century Jewish apocalyptic writing to set the scene for an Israeli-Palestinian conflict driven by satanic forces that unleashes chaos at the world's ending.

A New Kingdom
Week 4: Saturday

Matthew 13. 31-32

This parable, like many that Jesus told, conjured up for his listeners a picture they could immediately relate to. He was referring to one of their native species, and most people in the crowd would have been nodding in agreement as he described the tiny seed and tall tree. Maybe he even held up a seed between his thumb and forefinger and then pointed to one of the tall plants near to where he sat.

Every now and then, though, something happens which brings the parable alive for us modern readers, and that is exactly what happened for me with this story. I was privileged to be around at the beginning of something small and inconspicuous, some seventeen years ago. Sarah, a teacher in a school for autistic children and Francis, an occupational therapist, were both members of my church. These two women had noticed a growing number of children in the church who had additional needs, and who found children's ministry a significant, and sometimes impossible, challenge. They both had a concern to ensure that all our children were fully included in the life of the church. Together they began to plan what they could do to make a difference.

As they planned and prayed together, Francis heard God say that what they were beginning would be like a mustard seed – it would start small, but would grow, eventually affecting families outside the church. With that in mind, they named their project Mustard Seed.

Sarah and Francis shared their vision with the church, and soon they had a small team for each child, sometimes only two people, sometimes more if the child's needs were greater. The team members would take it in turns to support the child for a month each. They would sit with the family in church, sharing the task of looking after the child and helping him or her to participate in the worship. Then when the children went out to children's ministry they would accompany the child and give whatever support was needed to enable them to engage with the activities and hear the word of God in terms that they could understand.

For some children, this meant simply sitting with them, encouraging and prompting them to participate, explaining things and being on hand to take them for some time-out if it all became too much. For others, a more creative approach was needed. One little girl with microcephaly had individual sessions in a room by herself because she could not cope with being in a larger setting. Painstakingly, over 6 months, using all kinds of visual, tactile and other sensory methods, she was enabled to understand the story of Noah's Ark and God's love for Noah and, by extension, for herself. Sometimes, if a child really couldn't cope with being on the church premises all morning, or if something more was needed in terms of relationship-building, they could be taken to McDonalds, the park, or swimming.

Fast forward fifteen years. Sarah and Francis never lost sight of the original vision that their mustard seed would grow and extend beyond the walls of the church. With a growing team of volunteers, they began to offer support to families in the community, visiting them at home to give them strategies to understand their autistic children's behaviour and make life less challenging for them, which they do for increasing numbers of families. Then they began to run courses for parents and families, play therapy and sensory therapy, a six-week course teaching children strategies to manage anxiety, an occupational therapy service for additional needs children in local schools, and a siblings group where brothers and sisters could receive some individual attention away from their autistic sibling and in the company of people who 'get it'. God blessed them with funding and a venue tailored to their needs.

As the work has gone on expanding, their impact in the community has been tremendous. Parents have spoken of a lifeline being thrown to them, of being rescued when they could no longer cope. Recently the Mustard Seed Autism Trust was honoured by the local radio station and given its 'local heroes' award. No-one was surprised, except for Sarah and Francis, who had been just quietly getting on with what God had given them to do, and not looking for any particular reward.

So, though I may not, like Jesus' original hearers, be familiar with the tiny mustard seed and the tree it grows into, I have seen this kingdom principle at work – people who sowed an idea for something small that would bless some of the families in their church, and God took that tiny seed and grew it into something bigger than they ever imagined.

Now some of the families are meeting once a month on a Sunday with Sarah, Francis and a small team. While their children explore a Bible story through sensory play, the parents, in another room, are given space to explore faith in a safe, understanding environment. For many it may be the first time they have given much thought to the spiritual dimension of their lives. This is a recent venture, and is in its own way another tiny mustard seed of the kingdom of God. Who knows what He will grow from this one? Certainly they are like the birds of the parable, finding shelter in the branches of the tree.

I hope this story encourages you. I'm sure there must have been at least one person in the crowd with the lad who offered Jesus his packed lunch, who said, 'Five loaves and two fish? What on earth do you expect Him to do with that? Put it away and don't be silly.' But look what happened to his little offering once it was in the hands of Jesus. The same is true for you. Make a start on the first little task God has given you, and see what growth He will bring from it.

ROS BAYES

Ros has 10 published and four self-published books, and some 3 dozen magazine articles published. She is the mother of 3 daughters, one of whom has multiple complex disabilities. Her latest book can be found on Amazon.

rosbunneywriting.wordpress.com

A New Kingdom
Week 4: Sunday

Matthew 13:33

The kingdom of heaven is like yeast
The yeast smells clean, fresh, and crumbles easily.
It is alive, active, ready to start.

Yeast that a woman took and mixed
She rises early, lights the oven,
begins to sift flour and salt
through her fingers.
The texture is soft, dry, lifeless,
without smell or flavour.
She marvels at how it can be changed,
how tasteless grains
once bound with liquid yeast
can grow and stretch.

Mixed into about 30 kilograms of flour
The labour is hard,
kneading, turning, kneading.
Quietly, unnoticed,
she works the living yeast into each grain,
then waits.

Until it worked all through the dough
The dough begins to rise.

Again, she pounds the mix,
smoothing and folding.
Another time of waiting.

The dough rests and proves,
grows and moves to double its size.
She lifts it for a final working,
her hands shaping, pressing, caressing,
dividing the mixture,
preparing the loaves.
She sets them to bake.

Full of life and flavour
the bread is ready to share,
to feed, to spread its message.

SHEILA CLIFT
Sheila enjoys writing poetry and short stories. In 2009, she
won the *Jack Clemo* poetry award. She currently leads the
ACW Lancashire Group.

A New Kingdom
Week 4: Monday

Matthew 13: 47-50

Saturday Morning

With baby straddling my right hip, my left side shoved the rough old door into its stubborn frame and leaned hard against it. My free hand grabbed the worn brass key and turned the lock, around once, then frantically around once more, then a half turn, then out of the lock and up, and back upon the twisted hook. Shunting the heavy bolts hard into their casing, sacrificial specks of old lead paint rattled down in wild agreement. They fell to the ground landing among my angry tears, which lay there, shining like hot wet drops of blood upon the smooth red tiles.

Once indoors, his breathless crying calmed. I lifted his shirt to inspect the damage. Blood oozed from four small holes in his little belly. He repeated his tearful, certain statement: 'He poked me with a fork.' The evidence backed up his claim. The metal prongs had pierced the soft innocence of his delicate baby flesh, leaving a perfectly straight row of four deep, evenly spaced puncture wounds. Yards away from where I had stood washing dishes at my kitchen window, there in an enclosed, leafy suburban garden, on a lovely English summer's day, playing with older siblings and neighbour's children, my precious two-year-old baby boy had been deliberately stabbed.

And I was seething mad. A powerful protective, energy like nothing I had ever felt before surged within me. And on that day I learned, for absolute certainty, that I was capable of taking the life of another human being. For the next twenty-four hours, I initiated a total lock-down. I bolted all the doors, shut the windows, closed the blinds and stayed indoors, angrily pacing the floor, back, forth, back, forth, holed up with my children. I did this, not because I feared for my own safety, or for the safety of my children, but because I feared for the lives of my neighbours.

Discovering that I had, lurking somewhere deep within me, a powerful inclination to kill, to destroy life, in the interests of protecting my children, left me utterly shocked and stunned. Wrestling to keep the sheer primal force of it under control was exhausting. And yet, mixed in among the confusion and shock, I found a deeper understanding of how our Father in Heaven longs to protect us, His children.

On bad news days, and there have been plenty of late, God can seem absent, on the other side of the window, busy with something else. For me, this can raise questions about why evil is allowed to go unchecked upon this earth. I ask myself: 'Where was God in this?'

When evil seems to flourish, moral outrage and despair can set in and I press in harder, privately challenging God by asking Him: 'Why aren't you taking action to stop this? Why are you allowing this evil to continue?'

Sometimes it can seem to me, as if God has bolted the doors of heaven, and is pacing the floor angrily, back, forth, back, forth, holed up with the angels; as if He's holding back from releasing the full force of His wrath upon those who've dared to trespass on His patch, dared to harm His children.

In Matthew 13:47-50 Jesus clearly reiterates that there will come a day when He will take dramatic, irrevocable action to permanently protect His children from evil. On that day, He will unbolt the door of heaven and release His angels. First of all, the angels will separate the wicked from the righteous. In Matthew's account of Jesus' words, Jesus then goes on to say, without pausing for breath, that the very next action the angels will take is to throw the wicked into the fiery furnace. There will be no hanging about, no messing. The anxious waiting and wondering will be over, and all my difficult questions about the mystery of evil being allowed to flourish on the earth will be answered, with absolute certainty. I'm sure of it.

Prayers for wisdom

Lord, let me not shy away from difficult scriptures which can cause me to feel troubled and uncomfortable.

Lord, let me understand and accept your position of judgement as readily as I accept and understand your position of mercy, grace and forgiveness.

Lord, let me not turn my eyes away from these strong words in fear, but rather let me heed your warnings.

Lord, help me to accept and better understand why you must command your angels to separate the wicked from the righteous.

Lord, let me accept this angry part of you, the way you accept the angry parts of me.

Prayers for mercy and strength

Lord be merciful, let me lean in close to you; let me rest in your protective care.

Lord, give me the grace to pray for the wicked, and the strength to stand against them.

Lord, give me the grace to pray for victims of the wicked, and the strength to help them.

Prayers for patience

Lord, when I'm troubled by news of yet more evil, remind me that you have everything in hand, remind me of these verses, and though it's your wish that none will perish, you're planning to send the angels in, planning to oust those who harm your children. Lord when evil happens remind me that you are God, that you judge the hearts of men, that you are in control, and you will not let evil run unchecked.

And Lord, when my heart cries 'How long Lord? How long will you allow this?' remind me that you are watching, you are aware, you see it all too, you are poised on red alert, and you will return. At the end of the age your angels will descend upon the earth to do your will. There will be peace in that new place where the wicked are excluded. There will be no violence, no greed, no hatred, no wickedness. And there will be no thugs who stab toddlers in the tummy.

VAL FRASER

Val Fraser has a working background in journalism and communications. She was formerly the Communications Officer for the Diocese of Liverpool and worked on staff as the Creative Writer at United Christian Broadcasters (UCB). She currently supports the Communications Department at the Diocese of Manchester. Books: Val is the author of *Life in Cardigans*, *The Case for Cardigans*, *The Cardigan Diet* and the editor/designer of *Beyond the Banter*.

Twitter @ValFraserAuthor

A New Kingdom
Week 4: Tuesday

Matthew 13:24-43

As I pondered these verses, a childhood memory came to mind. My mother loved spending time in her garden. At every opportunity, she was out in the back or front garden; tending roses, cutting the grass, fluffing out the white alyssum, (should I say, 'white Alison' as it was called in our house?), or just staring at some unnamed piece of greenery.

When it came to weeds, there was a right way and a right time to pull them up. She would give a little side-to-side tug, and if it looked as if the weed had wrapped itself around the root of something else, she would leave it and come back to it at another time, from another angle. In these series of parables in Matthew 13, Jesus takes challenging Biblical truths and illustrates them with ordinary stories that his contemporaries and later readers would easily understand.

How many books, articles, discussions, debates and debacles have there been about what will happen in those last days? Jesus' simple gardening picture in Matthew 13:24-43 does not deal with the how and why. (I take that as my cue that I don't need to either.) Jesus simply tells us that it will happen.

So, what can we learn from this 1st Century Theological Gardener's Question Time?

The weeds have been there longer than we realise

It may surprise us when we find things lurking in the undergrowth of our life, but it doesn't surprise God. In this parable, the weeds have been growing almost since the beginning of the life of the wheat; underneath, getting rooted in. It's often the case that by the time we are aware of *weeds*, they've done a whole lot of growing and have become entangled around the *good wheat* of our life. God recognises the work of his enemy, but He has already seen the beginning from the end and so knows that it is better to wait before trying to get rid them.

We're going to need 'the patience of a saint'

It's a natural reaction of the servant to want to rid the wheat field of the weeds. Their instinct says to pull them up. However, their master is playing the long game. Immediate action would do more damage than good. They were going to have to wait.

How often do we ask God to deal with the weeds in our lives NOW! For me it is daily.

There are weeds, Lord... 'Let both grow together until the harvest.'

I'm worried about the weeds, Lord... 'Be still, and know that I am God.' Psalm 46:10

Tending this garden you've given me is hard, Lord... 'Count it all joy, my brothers, when you meet trials of various kinds, for you know that the testing of your faith produces steadfastness.' James 1:2-3

It's all going wrong Lord – 'And we know that for those who love God all things work together for good.' Romans 8:28

Can't you fix it now, Lord...? 'They who wait for the Lord shall renew their strength.' Isaiah 40:31

All these verses are from other places and contexts in the Bible, but I hope you can see with me, the overarching theme of patience and perseverance until THAT day.

Some flowers start off looking like weeds

In the parable, the owner knew immediately what had happened and who had done this to his field. The servants didn't. In the same way, God is fully aware of the difference between those plants that are for his purposes, and those that aren't. I do not have his knowledge, so I need to be careful.

There was another reason my mother didn't pull the weeds up straight away. It was because on occasion, she wasn't sure if they might be flowers. Hence the staring. She would be statuesque, her gaze fixed on one small plant. Often, she would leave it to see if it had potential to grow into anything better.

There are situations and people in our lives who may look like weeds, but they may just be slow to bloom. Every day that the Lord does not return, is another day of grace. It is not for me to know who and what will blossom in my life. In the meantime, it's another opportunity for us to tend the garden we've been given, giving everyone in it a chance to grow.

As we journey through this season of Lent, we may look upon the weeds in our lives and wish that they were not there; wish we could pull them out and throw them in the fire now. What might we miss if we do that? We might even benefit from their presence. God wants us to wait; who knows, maybe one of the weeds in our life just *looks* like a weed… it could produce a harvest more beautiful and fragrant than we'd ever imagined.

Memories of my mother's love and care for her garden have given me a fresh vision of God's love for me, as I grow in him. He holds our present growth and our future fulfilment in his hands. All he has purposed will come to fruition, and one day, like that harvest of good wheat, we will be gathered into his barn. Oh, what a day that will be!

Can it be today, Lord? Oh yeah, sorry, I forgot…

ANNEMARIE MILES

Annmarie is from Dublin, Ireland. She lives with her husband Richard who is a pastor in the Eastern Valley of Gwent, in South Wales. She writes short stories, magazine articles, devotional pieces for Christian radio, and blogs about her faith at www.auntyamo.com

Week 5:
A New Direction

Introduction

Jane Clamp

It wouldn't matter whether we were in the middle of something important. If an invitation was issued that promised to change our lives forever, wouldn't we jump in the car, set our satnav and be off?

This is pretty much what happened to the people we meet in this section. They encountered Jesus and heard his offer to 'Follow me.' It wasn't just the blind man who learned to see for the first time. All had their eyes opened once they met Jesus, and all saw life from a new perspective as a result. The path mapped out for them by circumstance or personal ambition and agenda was no longer the only one available. Following Jesus may have resulted in their making humiliating U-turns but, in doing so, they avoided a dead-end.

All learned that 'new life – this new direction – begins from the inside.'

Jane is creative writer in residence at BBC Radio Norfolk and on the Thought for the Day team at Premier Radio. She also preaches regularly and speaks at day conferences in which she also ministers through her saxophone playing.

A New Direction
Week 5: Wednesday

Matthew 4:18-22

The house here in Capernaum is quiet today. I like it like this. It gives me a chance to think. I'm sitting on the roof terrace, watching the sun sink over the waters of the Sea of Galilee, watching that familiar expanse become a glory of gold and blood-red, sparkling in the last, dying moments of the day. Then it's gone and grey eclipses the valley. I shiver. This is where it all began.

They say Simon is in Rome now – Peter I should call him, my son-in-law. I worry about him. There's been trouble, especially with the new Emperor, and Simon was never good at staying out of trouble. Always a strong, capable man, he built up the family fishing business from scratch. Everyone trusted him. Then Jesus came.

I remember that day. It wasn't quiet then. The town was buzzing with strangers. Jesus strode right past them, down to the water's edge, crunching across the shingle, air alive with creaking timbers, breaking waves and the lingering smell of fish. The men were there, crouching over their nets. There was no discussion, just a simple invitation to follow. Simon and Andrew dropped their tools, stood up and walked with Jesus to where Zebedee and his sons were working. It's as if Jesus had a kind of magnetism, a power, a presence that drew people to him. There was no need to ask questions. Actually Jesus never did say much when he wasn't preaching, but somehow he used the sort of language ordinary people understood. 'Come on,' he grinned to the fishermen, 'I'm going to show you how to catch people'. It was a special bond between them, not offered to anyone else. Jesus had that way of making you feel valued.

I know. Jesus came to me too, when I was in bed with a fever. I remember the burning, the wandering, the thirst. Then a cool hand on mine, like mountain ice melting in the sun, and the haze began to clear. I sat up. He spoke no words but I heard his call in my heart, like flames of love dancing. I would have done anything for him – but what? I couldn't go wandering off with the men. So I did the only thing I knew. I opened our home. I made it Jesus' home while he was in Galilee. He'd often pop in for a meal and an overnight stop. Then, when the weather was bad and they couldn't travel, he'd settle down for a while, doing odd jobs, fixing broken furniture while the lads went fishing. I loved that time. Afterwards, when Jesus had gone back to his Father and his friends scattered, there were still plenty of others seeking refuge: pilgrims, poor, persecuted believers – Christians they call themselves these days. All find welcome. Of course I'm old now. All I can do is sit and remember and when we gather together and tell our stories, I can't be certain I've got the facts quite right.

I do remember Simon's brother Andrew telling me that he met Jesus even before he came to Capernaum. Andrew had gone off with John the Baptist, a strange character by all accounts, somewhere in the south. This John was ranting away by the Jordan River when along came Jesus. 'Look, it's the Lamb of God,' said John, giving Andrew and his friend a strong hint to go and find out more. So they hung around with Jesus for a while.

'Well, what was Jesus like?' people ask. Andrew always said he was 'ordinary, yet extraordinary'. Yet, when Andrew returned to Galilee, he himself was different: unusually focused. The first thing he did was get Simon on his own and tell him about Jesus. I wasn't exactly listening but I distinctly heard him say 'We've found the Messiah.' Then he dragged his brother off to meet him. Would you believe it? Simon going to see a holy man! That's when they first started calling him Peter. Jesus again – changing things!

I don't know whether you've ever heard God calling you. Perhaps you think it sounds easy saying yes to God, but have you tried letting go and moving in faith? How do you know that the voice you hear really is the voice of God? And how can you bring yourself to say yes when, so often, you feel weak and unworthy? That was Simon's problem. He wasn't religious. He was just a rough fisherman, totally out of his depth, but Jesus wouldn't go away. One time he actually climbed into Simon's boat so he could teach the people more easily out on the waters. Afterwards, he asked Simon to let down the nets. Now they'd already been fishing all night and caught nothing, but Simon wanted to be gracious. He cast the nets over the side. Suddenly the waters began to boil and churn, nets straining, boat bucking and jerking. Other boats came to help land the impossible catch. Simon was overwhelmed. Jesus reduced him to a child, his strengths and skills apparently counting for nothing. 'Leave me alone,' he cried, 'I can't … I'm not good enough.' But Jesus raised him up, told him he was chosen. He would still be a fisherman but now he would catch people. So Simon Peter left everything and followed Jesus.

In the end, it's spending time with Jesus that makes the difference. That's what readies us to drop everything and go. Gradually we tune in to his voice, realise what he's asking. Often, it's not words we hear but something deep inside, a peace, a tugging at the heart. That's why I like to sit quietly here on the roof, listening. I can't do much these days but he still calls me. That's what I tell the folks who come here to worship and to break bread and remember. Jesus is still calling us to follow him.

APRIL McINTYRE

April McIntyre is a Reader at St. Michael's Church, Breaston in Derbyshire. She studied English at Sheffield University, completing a PhD on Dickens' novels. April currently writes for Derby Telegraph's Faith Files, reviews books for The Reader magazine, is a member of Derby Café Writers Group and enjoys creative spirituality.

A New Direction
Week 5: Thursday

Luke 19:1-10

I was at the top of the money tree. Zacchaeus – Jericho's eye-watering rich chief tax collector. Born and raised a Jew, I'd turned away from the faith of my forefathers, because who needs God when there's so much silver and gold there for the taking? The Roman Empire is a good paymaster, so I could have everything shekels could buy that a man could desire, especially once I'd creamed off the extra with my own tax surcharge. There's a knack to making money, and you can't fret about what it might cost other people. Nobody cared about me anyway – my acquaintances were mostly crooks and 'ladies of the night' and I know well that they only hung around for what they could get out of me.

I was known to be a swindler and a hard-hearted man. It's true, I thought nothing of walking over people to get to where I wanted. Did it bother me that I was cursed by the poor, despised by the priests and sneered at because of my height – or the lack of it? I held my head high whatever they said. And at least I was no hypocrite, never pretended to be a good person. Nothing was ever likely to change me into one – a twisted selfish guy like me. I certainly didn't expect mercy from God. There was surely a mounting debt I owed waiting for when I left this life. I can't take my riches to the grave. That's why I'm making the most of my money while I can.

My parents named me 'Zacchaeus'. It means 'pure.' A joke. Sadly, their innocent child strayed far away from following 'paths of righteousness for his name's sake' as the Psalms put it. I went in another direction that has been far more lucrative, and yet as time went by I felt empty, longing for something more. Instead of being my servant, money had made me its slave, and my lust for it was polluting my soul.

It was Matthew, the tax collector from Galilee who told me about Jesus. What with all the signs and wonders, the sick and demonised people made well and the extraordinary ideas he came out with, the word on the street was that he was a prophet – maybe even the Messiah. The day he met Jesus, Matthew simply walked away from the money and became one of his disciples! Matthew invited Jesus to his house, and he actually turned up – and was introduced to some of the worst sinners in town! I'd pay good money to have been there – the Pharisees were beside themselves with indignation, muttering into their beards about this outrageous Jesus; defiling himself by eating with such dregs of society. Yet here he was, this extraordinary preacher man who seemed to be the real deal, relaxing with a gang of lads who were getting more and more drunk and swearing a lot – frankly anything but religious!

Matthew's story made me wonder, was there a possibility that, bad as I was – and I mean really bad – this Jesus might want to talk to me? I knew I had to meet him – this healer of bodies and rescuer of souls.

Then one day I heard that he was heading towards Jericho. People were saying he'd restored the sight of that blind beggar who sits at the roadside on the outskirts of the city. So, casting aside my dignity and pride I hoicked up my robes and ran to join the crowd in search of a miracle of my own. Being short, I had to climb into a gnarled old sycamore for a good view of Jesus coming by.

Then – oh my days! He stopped right there and smiled up at me as if he'd known I'd be there all along. My heart was in my mouth and I nearly fell out of that tree because Jesus greeted me by name – and I had the uneasy feeling that nothing about me was hidden from him.

'Come down Zacchaeus!' he said, and as if that wasn't enough, he invited himself to my house – the same as had happened to Matthew! 'Yes Lord! It would be my greatest joy and honour to receive you!' I cried, and slid down the tree to land at his feet. People in the crowd I'd cheated for years were literally hissing with anger, others were speechless. They were all furious with me and disappointed at Jesus – didn't he know just what a despicable person I was? It's hard to be hated – even when you know you deserve it.

The news quickly spread, so several of my regular guests turned up for dinner too, dying of curiosity and happy to eat and drink at my expense. The religious types who'd drifted in seemed shocked to find themselves in the same house as many of Jericho's most notorious inhabitants. But nothing fazed Jesus. He even retold a parable about an arrogant Pharisee and a repentant tax collector praying in the temple; how God rejected the reverend's proud prayers and accepted the sacrifice of the sinner. That hit home.

At the end of the evening I made the speech of my life.

'Behold, Lord, half of my goods I give to the poor. And if I have defrauded anyone of anything, I restore it fourfold.' You could have heard a pin drop.

'Today salvation has come to this house,' Jesus replied, 'since he also is a son of Abraham. For the Son of Man came to seek and to save the lost.' I can't describe what that meant to me. It was as if I'd been born all over again. Jesus, the Lord of love, was inviting me to follow him in a wonderful new direction.

I didn't know then about that other tree, where Jesus would die to pay the debt I owed and show the way to heaven. It cost him his all and gave me everything.

CELIA BOWRING

Celia has worked with CARE (Christian Action Research and Education) alongside husband Lyndon for many years as a speaker and writer, especially on issues of prayer, and the value and dignity of human life. She has authored two books and written many articles, prayer resources and bible notes.

A New Direction
Week 5: Friday

Luke 15:11–32

Our passage is called The Parable of the Prodigal Son. It sits nestled amongst other teaching by Jesus, much of which he did through parables – or stories. The use of parable is very powerful, as it is a visual way of getting an idea across that grips the imagination. Jesus often used subject matter and language suited to his particular audience, and, in order to get the full benefit of the teaching, it can be useful to understand the cultural background.

In the parable we are looking at, I think the idea of inheritance is one that we still understand today, even though the way families live and work may be different. We see two brothers, one of whom is impatient to enjoy life to the full. In order to do this, he asks for his inheritance early. Imagine how that must have felt to his father – he is basically saying he wishes his father would hurry up and die so he can have his money. Although some fathers decided to divide up their estate before their death, that would have been at their discretion. The son is definitely overstepping the mark and disregarding his father's authority here.

A change of perspective

It isn't long before the son runs out of money, and the country he is in runs out of food. A hungry stomach focuses his thinking, and he realises he is worse off than his father's servants. For a Jew to be feeding pigs, which were seen as unclean, was a humiliation. The dire situation causes the son to make the decision that he will go home and ask if he can be a servant there.

I love the image of the father seeing him 'while he was still a long way off' (v20); his immediate response was to run to welcome his son. His kneejerk reaction is pure love, and we see him embrace and kiss his son – and then throw a huge party for him.

We are in that period of contemplation, looking towards Good Friday and Easter Sunday, when Jesus' ultimate sacrifice paid for us to enjoy everlasting communion with our heavenly Father. Just like the father in this story, God has provided the means for our salvation. He also gives us freedom, which means if we decide we want to go off exploring down our own path then we can. But, I am sure, most of us who have done that at some point recognise the safety and comfort that is found in being close to the Father. When we have moved away, if we come to him in repentance he welcomes us back with open arms.

Coming to our senses

While we can all see the stupidity and selfishness in the actions of the younger son, at least he came to his senses and recognised his need to acknowledge his foolishness.

Do we do that easily, or does it take a period of real difficulty for us to do so?

This son realised he was 'no longer worthy to be called [his father's] son' (v18). If we take time to dwell on our own lives, that can be a natural conclusion for us to come to also. We really don't deserve to be called God's sons and daughters. And yet, as long as there is no sin getting in the way, we have access to our Father at all times. Like the father in the story, God doesn't scrimp on what he gives to us. The dad gets the best robe – we have been clothed in Jesus' righteousness. He calls for a ring – this would have been a sign of being knitted back into the family (a signet ring carried the wearer's authority, and we carry God's too). In the way he responds to us, God continually celebrates the fact that, like the prodigal, we were once thought dead – but are now alive in him!

Begrudging or bitter?

I have always had a slight empathy for the other brother in this story – I wonder if you do too? He wasn't reckless like his younger brother. He remained faithful, working hard for his father (indeed he was still out in the field when his brother returned home). When he sees the fuss his father is making over his brother, he, somewhat understandably, gets riled by it all – especially the 'no expense spared' attitude. After all, he had remained at home, working diligently, but had never received so much as a goat to share with his friends (see v29).

Jesus was referring to the Pharisees in his description of this older son but, I wonder, do you ever respond to God with this kind of attitude? Perhaps you feel you have served him well for many years, and then along comes a young Christian full of character flaws and you watch while God seemingly blesses them – perhaps even with things that you have been longing for for years. Does your heart turn bitter or can you rejoice with them freely?

I find the following line really strikes to the heart of the matter: 'Son, you are always with me, and all that is mine is yours' (v31). That is so true, and yet we can so easily forget it. We can put our heads down, slog hard and grumble that we aren't having much fun. But is that more about our attitudes than about how God treats us? And are we any better than the prodigal when we act like this? How do we treat others who have turned away from God, then come back in repentance? Do we welcome them with love, or are we less than gracious?

During this day, why not take some time to check your heart – for bitterness or rebellion. If you feel perhaps you have been harbouring either, or both, then ask God for forgiveness – as well as his help to simply let it go. Then turn and rejoice before him, thanking him that he has made a way for us all – even the worst of sinners (and yes, the self-righteous among us too!) to come close to him as his children. Isn't that something worth celebrating?

CLAIRE MUSTERS
Claire is a freelance writer, speaker and editor, mum to two gorgeous young children, pastor's wife, worship leader and school governor. She is currently *Premier Christianity* magazine's freelance news and features journalist. Her latest of many books is *Taking off the mask: daring to be the person*

God created you to be. Find out more at www.clairemusters.com and @CMusters on Twitter.

A New Direction
Week 5: Saturday

John 4: 28-30

Does anyone share my problem of over-familiarity with Bible stories? I call it 'stained glass window syndrome'. Maybe it was compounded by childhood pictures of Jesus dressed in white, halo aloft, walking through meadows full of bright flowers and surrounded by angelic children. The challenge for me is to make those characters step down from the windows and out from the pages to appear as they really were – vulnerable and messed up, just like me!

The Bible incident about the woman at the well was truly shocking in its day. Only John recorded it – a measure of how hot it was to handle? Or was it just too mundane?

Imagine the tedium of the day: the stifling heat, weary travellers, thirst, hunger – and a woman in such disgrace that she had to fetch water when nobody was around. Jacob's Well was a notable historical setting, but this was hardly the stuff from which a story could be made to teach countless generations!

And yet it has been handed down and is a favourite. What did the nameless woman think when she saw a dishevelled Jewish man in residence at the well? Not her type – and neither would she be his! Samaritans were regarded by the Jews to be ethnically impure. Those who had not sold out to paganism insisted that God lived in their temple on mount Gerizim and not in Jerusalem.

They shared the same Abrahamic basis of faith, but there was simmering hatred between them.

Fully aware of all this, the woman must have recoiled when Jesus asked her for water. Whatever planet was this young man on? No doubt heartened by the fact that he was naive enough to converse, she pointed out that any water from her jar would make him ceremonially unclean. Did he not realise that Jews and Samaritans were racially incompatible and believed different things about God? Was he not aware of the megalithic social boundary he was crossing by speaking to her without her husband present?

But Jesus, unlikely Messiah in this humdrum situation, was in truth from another planet – or at least, from a place outside this one – and this tended to tilt the horizontal in unpredictable ways. Daily miraculous implementation of his mission statement was provoking an antagonistic response from the religious establishment – baffling in view of its provenance, straight out of Holy Scripture from the prophet Isaiah. Who could argue against proclaiming good news to the poor, crying freedom for prisoners, healing blind eyes and liberating those on the margins?

Not this woman for sure, but all she wanted was to fill her jar and return home.

Meanwhile, Jesus had recognised in her one of the blessed 'poor in spirit' who, aware of her brokenness, was a prime candidate for living water.

Several things happened at once.

The disciples returned, knowing her straight away for what she was. Still Jesus continued to offer her the gift of God – that never-ending living water leading to eternal life.

She abandoned all pretence. There was no hiding from Jesus' supernatural knowledge of her promiscuity and lack of husband. But in spite of seeing straight through her disreputable lifestyle, his eyes conveyed loving compassion. There was a growing awareness that his intention was not to shame her publicly. He was bringing her to the point of truth about her needy state – so she could open up to receive the living water!

The earthen water jar was abandoned. Back into town fled the outcast, no longer afraid to be seen, heralding the momentous news to all she met. Unconditional love had removed her shame and prompted the desire to share. She was travelling in a new direction!

I wonder how this scenario might play out today. Where would I have positioned myself? In whose shoes would I be standing?

As a gentile woman I couldn't have been a disciple in that original Jewish community, chosen by Jesus. But as a member of a twenty-first century mixed group of followers, would I have tried to protect Jesus by sending this 'undesirable' packing? She was clearly preventing him from taking the necessary rest and refreshment, bandying audacious words around. Might a sense of superiority have bubbled up, prompting me to take control?

She had crept out when no-one else from the town was around. Could I have been one of the townspeople who gave her a wide berth, or threw stones in angry self-righteous judgement?

Then there was the religious establishment. Jesus said he had not come to take anything away from the law – and it was crystal clear on adultery. Didn't these upholders of propriety have a point? Society needs rules for healthy living. Endless debate fodder here. So much easier to talk than walk. Would I have been tempted to display my advanced theological insights?

Then the woman at the well. Have I been guilty of looking for love in all the wrong places, of allowing myself to be defined by my sexuality alone? Have I tried to cover up things that don't bear the light of day? Do I hide behind masks?

How might Jesus have felt? We know he was fully human and must have been hungry and tired. The chosen disciples often acted like a bunch of misfits, failing to understand, jostling for power, turning people away. Constantly surrounded by eyes that didn't see and ears that failed to hear, the celestial prize upon which Jesus' gaze was fixed must have been of unimaginable beauty! How else could he have pursued his mission with such singlemindedness?

'If *only* you knew the gift of God…' What extravagant love!

Prayer

Dear God, please help me to let go of all my counterfeit 'goodness' and acknowledge my poverty before you.

Prepare my heart in true humility to receive that which I cannot earn and only you can give.

EILEEN PADMORE
Eileen has retired from a career in nursing, midwifery and academia. Current activities include creative writing, a prayer shawl ministry and membership of a missional community in down-town Leeds. Married for forty years to a professional musician, she is also main caregiver for her elderly mother.

A New Direction
Week 5: Sunday

John 9 35-38

You can read all you like. You can study all you like. You can look up things on Google and make notes and sit in lectures and talk and write learned notes and theses. You can run seminars. You can become a Very Important Person with Doctor in front of your name, and be invited to give lecture tours and tell other people what they need to know. You have arrived. You are somebody.

But maybe you know nothing.

All that knowledge is safely tucked inside your head and it's doing quite well there, thanks. It knows what it needs to know and even invites other people to tap into it if they like and take bits away. But there is a danger of disconnection if it doesn't reach the heart. The soul. If it doesn't tap into the emotions, the feelings, the red-raw messiness of human everyday life with its pain and its terror, its yearnings and its failures, and its hunger, hunger for something or Someone who can come in and bind up the wounds and heal. And whatever people say – that is what they want. However sorted and assured and capable and self-contained they look on the outside – inside everyone is screaming for connection, for belonging, to be held, to be secure and to know that they are loved.

This stuff has to be experienced. And that is exactly what happened to the blind man as Jesus passed by. Jesus didn't launch into a long explanation about why he was in that state. He didn't cite medical or spiritual opinions or query the man's history or conduct or attendance at the synagogue. He healed him. End of. He displayed what God is about. Compassion. Love. Healing. Forgiveness. Empathy, even on the Sabbath. Even on the Jews' most holy day – people came first.

Jesus said to the now not blind man, 'Do you believe in the Son of Man?' 'Who's that?' he asked, thinking it was his day for difficult questions and he'd quite like to get away and start looking at all the things he'd never seen. Jesus told him that he was looking at the Son of Man and it was he who was talking to him. Now this bloke didn't start a lengthy conversation about 'Who is the Son of Man?'. He didn't do the first century equivalent of Googling Son of Man versus Son of God. He didn't ask for a theological exegesis. He worshipped him. His insides reached out to Jesus and held on. Jesus had seen his need, his vulnerability, his acute, desperate pain, and healed him.

That's all he knew and all he needed to know.

Doesn't new life begin when we see – not only with our physical eyes but with our souls as well? Healing isn't ever just about the atoms and the cells and the blood and bones knitting together and restoring themselves, fighting sickness, chasing away disease. It is about those things – of course it is (ask any doctor) – but it's about much, much more. Jesus knew that. He knew that not only did this man's eyes need to see, but also that he needed someone to believe in, someone to worship. Someone who would save him.

Now the Pharisees didn't like this. All that mattered to them was keeping on the right side of their laws. So what if a miracle had just happened in the street? It was improper! It may be miraculous, but it couldn't be right, or acceptable to God, because it happened on their holy day. Surely a righteous God wouldn't stray outside the narrow confines of their prescribed protocols? Their God was firmly placed in a box, gift-wrapped with pink ribbon and stuck on a shelf so no-one would spoil the look by having the temerity to see what was inside.

Doesn't this make you want to weep? Don't you want to ask, 'What IS the matter with you? WHERE is your compassion? Here is a fellow human being who has been miraculously and instantly healed, and you'd rather stick to your treasured rules and policies than change your minds!'

Jesus wasn't into religion. I think he was into spirituality. I love the quote by Vine Deloria Junior, 'Religion is for people who are afraid of going to hell. Spirituality is for those who have already been there.' Spirituality – that spark in every one of us that reaches out and touches the divine, the spark which experiences the numinous. It may not be able to find words, or if finding, can't articulate them, but knows deep within the core of our being that the Other is present. We know therefore that we need not be afraid, because in all our brokenness we are held and loved and treasured.

'Only say the word and I shall be healed' says the Eucharistic liturgy. By a word, this man was healed in body, mind and soul. He saw Jesus. Everything for him was different. It was a new direction in every sense for him. He didn't have to be afraid. It was okay.

All the rules and regulations in the world won't do this for us. All the strategies and the ticky-boxes won't hold and comfort. Our outside is held together by our insides.

New life – this new direction – begins from the inside. It's adoring the God who made us, who restores and refreshes us, who continues to sustain us throughout our lives, in every way, as we fix our eyes upon our Saviour.

And we are truly healed, as we gaze upon him.

EIRENE PALMER

Eirene enjoys her voluntary work as Diocesan Spiritual Adviser for the Diocese of Derby. She is also a spiritual accompanier and runs courses on aspects of spirituality. Her other passions are music, choir, family and writing. She is currently published by BRF and Woman Alive, and co-runs ACW Café Writers in Derby.

A New Direction
Week 5: Monday

Acts 9:20-22

The boy stood at the side of the swimming pool. He looked down at the water. Splash! The water rippled as someone jumped in. The boy watched as they plunged beneath the surface and then re-emerged, laughing and shaking water from their eyes. It looked like fun! The boy reminded himself that he was fine just as he was. Standing at the edge. Watching. He'd never jumped into the water, ever. He couldn't do it. It was too scary. Yes, people made it look like fun, but surely, they were wrong. Jumping in? Leaving the safety of the side of the pool? Crazy. The boy shook his head slightly as he sensibly slid into the water, never letting go of the edge.

The next week, the boy stood at the edge of the pool. Other people jumped in. The boy began to slide into the water, when a voice called his name: 'Jump! Come on, I'm here.' The boy looked at his father, standing in the pool. He looked at the water. He looked at his father again. Without looking away, he jumped. As he re-emerged, the boy was shaking his head. He was shaking water from his eyes. And he was laughing.

For a long time, Saul stood away from what Jesus was doing. Refusing to join in. These people finding joy through discovering that Jesus is God? They'd got it wrong. Crazy lot.

Saul was against Jesus, and anything to do with Jesus, with every fibre of his being.

Until a voice said his name.

Saul asked, 'Who are you?'

'I am Jesus.'

And I am here.

With you.

In Saul's antagonism, his anger, his fear, his hatred,

Jesus came to him,

exactly where he was,

and spoke his name.

In your situation,

exactly where you are,

Jesus comes to you.

And He speaks your name.

Don't be scared.

Isaiah 43:1b Fear not…I have called you by name.

Saul met Jesus, and Saul was changed.

No longer did he have to be the person he used to be.

Jesus released him from being bound by the past.

John 8:36 if the son (Jesus) sets you free, you will be free indeed.

Don't be a prisoner to your past; whether yesterday, last week, years ago….

Dare to let go.

Be released into your present.

A present with Jesus-whispers echoing through it:

I'm here.

So Saul, grasping that 'I am Jesus' is with him, has the courage to tell people what he's discovered:

'Jesus is the Son of God.'

What have you discovered about Jesus?

Who is he to you?

Do you have the courage to tell people who Jesus is to you?

Maybe you think you can't; it's too difficult, too scary, you'll get the words wrong, people will laugh…

Is it possible that Saul thought the same thing?

Possible that Saul thought he couldn't?

Yet, as he stood there and simply told people who he'd discovered Jesus to be, what happened? 'Saul increased in strength.'

And he carried on telling people.

And his strength grew even more.

As we learn who Jesus is,

as we tell others who Jesus is,

as we remind ourselves who Jesus is,

we'll grow in strength.

Later, Saul (who changed his name to Paul),

the man who others respected and admired;

the man who boldly stood in front of people and told them about Jesus;

the man who evangelised and established the early church;

wrote about his strength (2 Corinthians 12).

A strength

found in

weakness.

Something, maybe, he'd started to learn when he first plucked up courage to tell people about Jesus:

'When I am weak....'

Sometimes we do feel weak.

We feel frustrated by our limitations.

We can't go on.

Our strength has gone.

We're struggling.

Other people may not see it.

But we do.

'...then I am strong.'

Paul's weakness was his strength.

When he realised that, he wanted weakness more and more.

His weakness was a good thing.

Because it kept his eyes on Jesus.

Jesus who said to him,

Jesus who says to you:

'My grace is sufficient for you, for my power is made perfect in weakness.'

Jesus called Saul by name.

When he heard it, Saul let go of clinging to the edge of what he thought he knew.

And reached for what he now knew for certain.

Jesus here.

With him.

Always.

Hebrews 12:1&2 Therefore… let us also lay aside every weight… and let us run with endurance the race that is set before us, looking to Jesus…

Prayer

Father God,

I can be like that boy in the swimming pool.

Clinging to the edge.

Not daring to jump.

Scared to reach for the freedom you offer.

Thank you that you call my name.

It amazes me that you even know my name.

Yet you do know it.

And you know me.

You know my weaknesses.

Help me to know your strength.

Amen.

EMILY OWEN

Emily Owen grew up in Leicester. Aged 16, she was diagnosed with a rare neurological condition, Neurofibromatosis Type 2, which has led to numerous operations and left her deaf. Emily speaks at meetings and events, both Christian and secular, and enjoys sharing her life experiences. Emily has written 6 books to date, one being her memoir *Still Emily: Seeing rainbows in the silence* and the other five in her devotional *30 Days* series.

New Life – 165

A New Direction
Week 5: Tuesday

Luke 23:39-43

'I woke to find myself in a dark wood,
Where the right road was wholly lost and gone.'
(Dante, Divine Comedy, Inferno)

There stood a dark wood at the place of The Skull outside
the city of Jerusalem on that day. Golgotha, as the
Hebrew speakers called it. Three trees threw grotesque
shadows across the hill, the disfigured shapes of arms
nailed to branches and breathless bodies hanging taut on
trunks. The crowd milled in the shadows of the trees,
darkening them further with their scorn and mockery,
hearts as hard as the timber which held the three men
captive.

It is here in this malevolent place one of the men awoke,
stirring from the depths of spiritual somnolence. The
right road had been lost a long time ago and he had
travelled far in the wrong direction ending here at
Golgotha, now a law breaker convicted, sentenced and
dispossessed of hope.

The final steps of his journey to this destination had been
shared with the one who hung on the adjacent cross,
silent despite the insults being flung at him by the Jewish
leaders, the people, the soldiers and the third condemned

offender. As he listened to the man called Jesus pray for the forgiveness of those who drove nails into his hands and feet and heard them mock him for being the Christ of God, the Chosen One, there came the realisation that a heinous injustice was being committed against a person who should not be here at all. This silent man on the tree surrounded by law breakers had broken no law and had never strayed from the right road. Here in this dark wood was someone who did not deserve to be executed, an innocent soul in a place of condemnation and death.

As the fog of insensibility finally left the criminal's mind, his eyes were opened to reality and the truth gave him courage to speak.

> *'...we are receiving the due reward of our deeds;*
> *but this man has done nothing wrong.'*
> (Luke 23:41)

Into the tumult, truth rang out from the lips of an outcast. It was a declaration of the human condition and about Jesus Christ who hung in stark contrast to it all.

As he turned his head, one condemned man to another, the criminal submitted to the truth and accepted it with humility, recognising the need to fear God. With the understanding that God's Kingdom belonged to the man into whose eyes he now looked, he expressed his belief in the possibility of redemption, confessing hope and faith.

> *'Jesus, remember me when you*
> *come into your kingdom'.*

The man saw in his final hours of life, the light that shone in the darkness, illuminating the road that had been lost to him. In that moment, he changed direction.

> *'That light doth so transform a man's whole bent*
> *That never to another sight or thought*
> *Would he surrender, with his own consent;*
> (Dante, Divine Comedy, Paradiso)

Light broke through the trees as the Son of God spoke words of loving acceptance and promise that the man surely had never imagined he would hear. His journey would not end there on the tree.

> *'Truly, I say to you, today you*
> *will be with me in paradise.'*

Even in those last hours enduring terrible pain and suffering, he found the right road and it would lead to heaven. He would assuredly remain at Jesus' side from that very moment.

Approaching Easter, the fell shadows of the dark wood grow long and shroud us all, the law breakers. We stand on the hill, violators of divine statute, contemplating the chilling horror of Golgotha's trees.

In a merciless and contemptuous world that continues to hammer, mock, jeer and scorn Christ, the words of the crucified criminal still reverberate in the shadows, challenging and rebuking us – punishment is our due reward but Jesus has done nothing wrong. Witnessing the profound humility and grace of Jesus on the cross through enlightened eyes is an invitation to experience a quickening of spirit. Such an encounter with Christ has the power to awaken us to the truth and to open our eyes.

Redemption begins with submission and the road to paradise is followed with humility in the belief that Jesus is the only one who can bring us into his Kingdom. The transformative power of the divine light means that we experience an entire reorientation of heart, mind and soul. A new journey begins, as we travel in a new direction out of the darkness of sin and unknowing, believing in the truth that will give us courage to speak in the face of the world's deep hostility and enmity.

To follow the road in the footsteps of the criminal on the cross and the countless others who have believed in the Messiah is to live out the paradox that in surrender there is liberation.

We are journeying in hope from the depths of the dark wood to the heights of Paradise, towards pure truth, grace and love.

'My will and my desire were turned by love,
the love that moves the sun and the other stars'.
(Dante, Divine Comedy, Paradiso)

JULIE BROWN
Julie enjoys writing at newpebbles.blogspot.com, sharing thoughts on her journey in words and faith. An ACW member since January 2017, she is from Northern Ireland living with her husband and two sons near Lisburn.

Week 6:
New Commandments

Introduction
Wendy H. Jones

In Exodus 20 God gives Moses the Decalogue, or Ten Commandments. These pointed to the way in which the Israelites should live their lives. It is believed that these were a summary of the law which was yet to come. The importance of these is that they came directly from God himself.

We still follow these principles today and English and Scottish Law is founded on these. As principles, they demonstrate how we should live our lives as moral human beings.

However, we are no longer bound by all the intricacies of Old Testament Law. Through Jesus' birth, death and resurrection he demonstrated we could have New Life, a life based on love and relationship with him.

Wendy is the author of the award winning *DI Shona McKenzie Mysteries*. Her Young Adult Book, *The Dagger's Curse*, was a finalist in the *Woman Alive Magazine* Readers Choice Award 2017. She is the webmaster for ACW and attends City Church Dundee, where she runs the ACW writing group, City Writers.

New Commandments
Week 6: Wednesday

Matthew 5:38-39

You have heard it said, 'An eye for an eye and a tooth for a tooth.' But I say to you, do not resist the one who is evil. But if anyone slaps you on the right cheek, turn the other also.

My first memory of 'turning the other cheek' comes from years ago in the school playground. I had been hit by another child and I have a fleeting recollection of thinking I shouldn't hit back. Happily, my assailant ran off and I wasn't put to the test! After another similar encounter I didn't return the blow, but sadly refused any later conciliation.

My teenage years coincided with the beginning of World War II, the occupation of Europe and a real possibility of an invasion of Britain. My recurrent nightmare was of being captured for enemy interrogation. The example of Jesus healing the dying slave of a Roman centurion, a sympathetic man, but still a member of the hated enemy occupier, never touched my thinking; nor that God's family could include the Nazis.

Later there were voices of compassion for the sufferings of the German people. When I was seventeen I went to a Bible study group where the leader deplored the ruthless bombing of Dresden, especially the old city and the cathedral. It was a view debated well after the war, and in 1959, born out of their common sufferings, Coventry was twinned with Dresden, in an act of mutual reconciliation.

The views expressed in this Bible group may have helped me later to befriend a German prisoner-of-war. He was one of a number who had been working on local farms and were now given some freedom of movement. This enabled me to have an occasional talk with one of them. I gave him a small book before his eventual return to the war-torn city of Leipzig.

As a student, I came face-to-face with the New Commandment in a very radical form. I had a particular friend who was a Quaker. Through her I learnt about The Religious Society of Friends and their views of total non-violence, most members refusing to bear arms and go to war. I agreed with so many of their precepts, though I couldn't accept that final principle. But Easter week reminds us so potently of Christ's refusal to use violence when facing death. Instead he gave comfort to a fellow sufferer, and to us, forgiveness.

As a young adult, I came to appreciate the value of passive resistance as a means of confronting evil without returning violence for violence. This was particularly true during the anti-apartheid period in South Africa. At that time, I was offered the opportunity of living in South Africa, but because of my new work I never did so. I wondered later whether I would have been brave enough to join the anti-apartheid movement by joining the Black Sash Women, for instance. They defied predominant public attitudes by supporting this cause and human rights in general, winning the praise of Nelson Mandela.

In the early 1960s our local church did give us an opportunity to combat racial prejudice, when we were asked to offer hospitality to someone of a different ethnic background. I don't think anyone of a darker skin had ever been seen in our suburban area at that time. I had expected as our guest an Indian lady, preferably wearing a colourful sari, who would instantly delight our two young daughters. I was shaken to find that it was actually a six-foot Nigerian gentleman, who, in height at least, threatened to overwhelm our small family. But his genial personality quickly broke down any barriers and Mr. George, or rather 'Uncle George', as our children called him, visited us on further weekends before his eventual return to Nigeria. I was aware of nervous twitching of curtains though, when we walked to church along our silent streets on Sunday mornings. I learnt later of the apprehension felt by our neighbours following these visits. But meeting Mr. George was for us a very rewarding encounter. His kindness, particularly to the children, showed the power of love to vanquish fear, itself so often a root cause of violence. While not a direct analogy to the workings of the New Commandment this unexpected friendship seemed to me closely allied to it.

But it was much later as a Sunday school teacher that I considered the New Commandment at another level. I wrote a playlet for children set against the traditional Easter custom of 'egg-rolling.' The main character, Jenny, learns how her own insensitive behaviour provoked bad feeling in her former best friend, Susan Green.

Jenny returns home complaining bitterly to her mother that her egg was deliberately bashed up by Susan in the egg-rolling game.

'Well, you did upset Susan, boasting about reading your poem out in assembly last week. Do you remember, dear? – when she was so disappointed at being a runner-up'.

'Mum, that's different! But I do know she tried hard with her poem. She told Judy Anderson that the harder she tried the worse it got. The words just wouldn't come right! Mine seemed to just spring out of my head. I told her so'

'Jenny! That didn't make her feel any better, I'm sure, and perhaps you haven't heard Susan's father has lost his job; they may have to leave the village.'

'Oh, poor Sue, she never told me!'

Jenny quickly agrees to take an Easter egg round to Susan as a peace offering.

Just a glance at Jenny's little quarrel is enough to make me realise how rarely I have understood a conflict from the other's point of view; how often my own behaviour has been the hidden cause of dissension. Now, in very old age, I can see that it is only by God's extraordinary grace that some long-standing difficult relationships have grown into something loving. For the rest, I can only beg forgiveness. It seems to me that we can only try to follow Christ's New Commandment, fail and try again, but on succeeding I believe we catch a glimpse of the peace of heaven.

MARGARET GREGORY

Margaret's life has always been centered around her family, her parental family, and now her own. The older generation, especially, reared her in the Christian faith. Language studies later nurtured a love of words and a need to write. Her faith has often offered the material and inspiration for writing.

New Commandments
Week 6: Thursday

Matthew 5:40-42

'Mum, we just wondered if the idea of finding a house big enough for us, my business and you, is something you'd consider.'

My daughters question was completely unexpected. My husband had died suddenly three years previously and I was still living in the four-bedroomed family house. It was too big; I was lonely and didn't like living alone. Now a new option came tantalisingly into view. What should I do?

First, I panicked. There were so many things to consider. What about my other children? The arrangements needed to be fair. I had heard of desperate family arguments and split-ups based on inheritance issues, and I wanted to avoid that. I sounded each child out. Would they be happy if I moved in? There were questions we needed to look at, but I needn't have worried. Their first consideration was for me. Was this what I wanted? In which case go ahead. So, after a time of prayer and consideration, I agreed and the search began.

My daughters house sold immediately and so she, her husband, two children and two cats plus what seemed a huge amount of furniture for her business, moved in with me. Everything seemed to be progressing smoothly and I naively wondered if, because we had offered all our plans to God, things would continue smoothly.

Two months later, I had a buyer for my house; we had found THE ONE for us; the future looked promising. Then, suddenly things began to fall apart.

In the space of six weeks, my house sale fell through; my son-in-law lost his job and my daughter found she was pregnant. 'What next?' I wondered, my mind reeling. It had all felt so 'right' and we were committed to this pathway. There seemed no option but to carry on.

When our venture began, back in the spring, we expected that we would be moved by September, making my grandchildren's transition to a new school easier; but as September loomed we realised this was not to be. The five-mile school run back to their old school became part of their new routine. The thought of them having to change schools twice was just a step too far.

The baby was due in the middle of November and as each week passed I grew more concerned. My house had a prospective buyer; an offer for a new/different house had been accepted but what was described by the estate agent as 'A chain-free, straight-forward transaction' became increasingly complicated each week. Every time a date for completion was mentioned, another problem was highlighted and a new wait began.

Eventually at the beginning of November a date of completion was offered. At last we were moving! We were excited but our high spirits evaporated when our solicitor rang on the day of exchange. She sounded upset. 'I'm sorry,' she began, 'I have bad news. The party at the beginning of the chain has rung to say they will only exchange if £5,000 is taken off the price.' 'I have to tell you,' she continued, 'I am dismayed. This behaviour is very unethical.'

It was as if we were sitting directly under a storm cloud. All the waiting, all the negotiations, all the expectations, now meant nothing. How had this happened? How had we got to this stalemate? I felt let down and deceived and I was angry. More importantly what should we do? We asked for time to 'think'. My daughter contacted the next party in the chain, to tell her what had happened and how, at this late stage, it might all fall through. She broke down and cried saying 'I'm not sure I can go through all this again.'

Our house was very quiet that evening as we each pondered on the situation. Just when I thought I might explode if I couldn't calm all the contradicting thoughts that flooded my mind, I recalled some verses of Scripture. Jesus was speaking at the end of the passage that we know as 'The Sermon on the Mount'.

If anyone would sue you and take your tunic, let him have your cloak as well. And if anyone forces you to go one mile, go with him 2 miles. Matthew 5:40-41

We weren't being sued but the principle seemed the same. Jesus was saying if someone asks for something from you, give it and even give more than was asked for. I was feeling hurt and angry. I wanted revenge, to show those people that we weren't naive, that they could not treat us in this way. But Jesus seemed to smile and say, 'It's ok; give it. God understands. Give Him your anger too.'

So, I called a family meeting and told them what I had felt. I read them the passage from Matthew's Gospel. I'd done my sums and I did have the money available. We decided to ring the solicitors in the morning to find out if there had been any new developments, and if they confirmed our fears, to tell them we would pay the difference. We rang to reassure the next party in the chain and when she heard that I was prepared to pay, if that meant we could then move, she offered to pay half.

The contracts were signed and two weeks later, on a Monday we moved in. Three days later, my daughter gave birth to a beautiful baby girl.

Five years have passed and our house is now a home; it has seen many changes. But one thing has not changed; we are grateful for that lesson of Grace. The King we follow has rules that may seem like foolishness to this world, but in His Kingdom of Love they make perfect sense.

MARION ANDREWS

Marion is a mum/grandma/widow/retired nurse who writes for 1000 reasons. She mainly does this to express things she is passionate about like Jesus, our wonderful world, injustice, those she loves and the NHS. Her novel Angels of the NHS, documents her experience as a student nurse in London in the 60's and is available via Amazon.

New Commandments
Week 6: Friday

Matthew 5:43-48

'But...' 'So...' 'For...' 'If...' It's the little link words that count. Jesus uses them in this passage and it's uncomfortable. He is talking to his disciples, an inner group amongst a crowd of people who've gathered on a hillside. All are curious to see and listen to the man who's taking the neighbourhood by storm with his extraordinary behaviour and startling words. He hasn't finished yet. Time after time, subject after subject, he challenges current thinking with outlandish sayings that require folk to sit up and listen. Imagine you're one of his rookie disciples. You listen to Jesus' words and think them through:

'You have heard it said...'

Who said it? Ah yes, our Jewish teachers. They know the Law and we've grown up listening as they pass it on to us.

'You shall love your neighbour and hate your enemy...'

Yeah, yeah. We know that. We love our friends and our nation, even our religion, for all its rules and regs. And we hate those who don't fit into our worldview. We're doing OK!

'But...'

Uh, oh. There's more?

'I say to you...'

Have our teachers got it wrong? Can Jesus' word override all those other words we've learnt? I guess if he's God his word is gospel.

'Love your enemies...'

What? Why? How? You expect me to review my attitude and show compassion, kindness, and courtesy? What about those who treat me badly?

'Pray for those who persecute you...'

You're kidding, right? Why should I pray for them?

'So that you may be sons of your Father.'

I can be one of God's family, a child of the Almighty God? That's some special family!

'Who is in heaven...'

God is in control, overlooking his world, and yet he seems to be here too – in the form of this man Jesus.

'For he makes the sun rise on the evil and on the good and sends rain on the just and on the unjust.'

It seems that the grace and love of the Creator of the universe beams down on everyone irrespective of who they are and what they do.

'For if...'

Two more little words. What's coming next?

'You love those who love you...'

Yes, I love those who love me. I'm OK there.

'What reward do you have?'

Oh, isn't it good enough to love my loved ones?

'Do not even the tax collectors do the same?'

You're saying they actually have friends to love?

'And if you greet only your brothers...'

Perhaps I do exclude the lonely and unloved. Hm. This is getting more and more uncomfortable. Has he nearly finished?

'What more are you doing than others?'

Not a lot, to be honest.

'Do not even the Gentiles do the same?'

Outrageous! I'm a Jew. Don't talk to me about Gentiles!

'You therefore must be perfect...'

Fat chance. Oops... I hope he can't read my thoughts.

'As your heavenly Father is perfect...'

God is perfect and I need to be like him. That's some ask.

Well, our imaginary disciple is honest, if nothing else. What about us? How do Jesus' words affect our thinking and behaviour? What steps should we take to change our attitude to other people? Each person is made in God's image and is loved by him. Do we treat all people with respect and honour? Can we look for the good in those who wish, or do, us harm? Can we have compassion and use courteous words for those who post vitriolic comments on social media, or whisper unkind things behind our backs? Can we show our allegiance to Jesus the Peacemaker with words and acts of peace, and welcome the opportunity to do good? Can we remember that it is not our place to judge others? Can we pray for our persecutors, as Jesus did? Forgive them, Father, for they know not what they do. (Luke 23:34)

God expects us to do more than indulge our natural inclination and personal interest. We are to look out for the lonely and marginalised. We should share with others what we know and experience of Jesus. We need to listen and love and act on God's behalf with the people we meet each day. Check: Can God be seen in me?

Jesus lived and died for us. He shows us how to live responsibly with the privilege of being God's children. Let's serve him faithfully, however testing it may be for our human psyche. And be thankful that we have God's Spirit to help us.

PAM POINTER

Pam is the author of a dozen non-fiction and poetry books and also writes meditations, features and columns for various publications. Her latest book, *Help! I'm a New Mum!* is published by Kevin Mayhew Ltd. More info on the book, plus blogs, photos and poems, are on Pam's website (http://pampointer.wordpress.com/).

New Commandments
Week 6: Saturday

Matthew 20: 25-28

Imagine, if you can, how Jesus and His twelve chosen followers actually lived day by day. Who, you might ask, could possibly offer B & B to thirteen men – and possibly a few others – let alone Dinner? Offers of hospitality must have come from folk who heard Jesus preach His message of God's love and been impressed. Impressed and curious. It would have been a few generous Jewish families who would have taken one or two of this itinerant group of cheerful odd-bods, who had something of the refugee about them, into their houses, ply them with questions and food, and no doubt recount stories of their own.

The incident of James and John and their mother looks to me as though it happened one morning. There was a lapse in time before the other ten disciples heard what the sneaky trio had asked of Jesus. They then had time to chunter:

'Blooming nerve.'

'Who do they think they are?'

'What a cheek!'

'Why them?'

'How dare they ask for favours behind our back.'

'*!+/<^>*@)(0'\-±!'

'Now now, Andrew,' says Peter, 'Mind your language. You're not on our fishing boat now.'

Later, as it was beginning to get dark at about 6 o'clock in the evening, they would have dispersed to the homes of the kind hosts who had offered them shelter. It was after this that Matthew records the intriguing words 'Jesus called them to him.' Other translations say 'Jesus called them together.' Either way if they needed to be called together or to Him, they were manifestly not already together or with Him. My suspicion is that a sheepish James, John and their Mum were sent by Jesus to track down the other ten disciples [news travels fast in small communities] and ask them to gather, maybe under a conspicuous tree or in an inn. The Lord wanted a word with them.

Jesus must have felt that the issue had to be dealt with before they would meet together again the next day. It was that serious. Teaching them their need to cultivate the attributes of a servant and rid themselves of all desire to be privileged was a matter of vital concern. He could not allow His beloved band of close followers to chat the night away with their hosts without getting this lesson embedded first. Resentment towards James, John and their mother needed sorting too:

> Some things in the Christian life need addressing now, as in NOW, not tomorrow.

> We are servants.

> Are you always kind to your neighbours?

If you are not sure who your neighbours are, let the parable of the Good Samaritan (Luke 10:30-37) speak to you and set you thinking. Its brevity and depth are among the finest short stories ever told.

He (the man who had asked Jesus who his neighbour was) said 'The one who showed him mercy.'

And Jesus said to him, 'You go and do likewise.'

If this parable needs reinforcing read a few more of Jesus' words, this time in Matthew 22:36-40.

Teacher, which is the great commandment in the Law?

And He (Jesus) said to him, 'you shall love the Lord your God with all your heart and with all your soul and with all your mind. This is the great and first commandment. And the second is like it. You shall love your neighbour as yourself. On these two commandments depend all the Law and the Prophets.

It is a little unsettling to be told that we are to be servants to our neighbours, and love them; but Christianity is unsettling – and enriching.

ROBIN CARMICHAEL
Now a retired doctor, Robin was converted to Christianity from a half-baked agnosticism when a student. He enjoys freelance writing and has had stuff published mainly in magazines. His wife, two sons and their families give him much joy – mostly. His zaniest hobby is astronomy.

New Commandments
Week 6: Sunday

John 13: 12-17

Wash One Another's Feet

The water seemed cool, refreshing,
As he knelt before each one of them
Tenderly washing, then drying, each weary pair of feet.
Lifting his head, he looked into each familiar pair of
eyes,
Before quietly rising and moving on,
Pausing only to talk with Peter, who, true to form,
Had something to say on the matter.

So simple;
So strangely unexpected, as they shared the Passover
lamb together;
But this act of Jesus soothed the strain that had been
growing,
Between them and among them.

Then came the question.

'Do you understand what I have done for you?'

Silence.

They looked at one another but could not answer.

Jesus knew his time had come.
Deep down, so did they.

Gently, Jesus explained.
They listened intently, knowing how important this
must be.

He spoke to them about their life together.
How things would be among those who truly followed
him;
Those who were changed by his example.

He, their Teacher and Lord, had washed their feet.
Love is like that.

'You also ought to wash one another's feet.'
Not just giving service but graciously receiving it too.
Humility is like that.

Slaves serve because they have to.
It is what they do.

Jesus' followers have loving service as their pattern.
It is who they are.

2.

'Wash one another's feet'?
Irrelevant.
Outdated
Or so it may seem.
Yet,
Within these words

There is a new commandment still,
As ripe and fresh for picking now, as then.
Timeless truth to tell.

Humility displacing pride;
Care instead of apathy.
Love within community
Nobody forgotten.

Jesus' example given,
That, in each age,
Even this age,
All might learn anew to do what he did then.

3.

Lord, today,
Open my eyes that I may see the needs of others;
Quicken my will to respond when I am able.
Give me grace to accept help when it is offered to me.
May all that I think and say and do, this day,
Be shaped and seasoned by your love.
In Jesus' name, I pray,
Amen.

SANDRA PICKARD
Sandra Pickard is a retired URC Minister, a wordsmith, who fashions words into poetry, short stories, meditations and whatever else comes to mind.

New Commandments

Week 6: Monday

John 13:34

It had been a long day, but time was short now and there were deep life-giving words that had needed to be said, for there weren't many days left.

Jesus lay back, looking up at the stars hanging over that quiet corner of Bethany's dark sky, remembering those first stars that burst into life across a virgin sky, creating night out of the dark void; recalling the bright star that had hung over a stable.

His thoughts shifted from the night to the day. A day of contrasts it had been in many ways; a day where love and pain mingled; a day where beauty and ugliness walked side by side.

He smiled as he remembered the scene at dinner: Martha her usual busy self, pouring her love like a marinade into the food she created for her guests, making them feel at home while still keeping an eye on the pots over the fire; Lazarus looking round the room, his senses alive and alert to the sights and sounds of friends and neighbours who had gathered to see him – a man who had tasted death and was now determined to drink in and delight in and marvel at the fullness that new life could offer, whether for an hour, a day, a week or a year.

And then there was Mary. Dear Mary. Deep Mary. So often she had sat at his feet in that little house in Bethany, the closest to a home that he had known these past years. Amongst all the people who would gather there, she was almost an unseen listener in this room, first soaking up his words, and then allowing them to envelop her, enfolding her like a shroud. It was almost as if she knew. Long before he uttered that new life-giving commandment to the others he had found himself whispering – as if to try out the sound of those precious, simple, God-filled words of sacrifice: 'Mary, love one another, just as I have loved you.'

Today love had been poured on his feet; the sweet smell of nard drenched with love, yet infused with the pain to come. The oil of blessing mingled with the oil of burial rolled across his foot and pooled like amber blood between his toes. Mary unthinkingly doing the unthinkable by letting down her hair and sweeping it like the long smooth curtain that would later be torn in two, to and fro across his feet, anointing his skin. Jesus wondered if the jar of oil had been opened and used for Lazarus at his burial, the rest kept and now seeping across the floor in that same house.

Judas's bullying words had sliced viciously through the fragrant aroma, drawing them away from the tender scene, dismissing the lavish generosity of the gesture, demanding why the perfume had not been sold and the money given to the poor, deflecting away from the act of genuine love.

Betrayal, bullying and blessing twisted together in that moment like the intertwined flax of the rope that Judas would later seek out.

'Leave her alone,' Jesus had said and leaned closer to Judas as he whispered softly: 'Judas, love one another, just as I have loved you.' The words falling from his lips to the floor and lying abandoned in the pool of oil. He knew that the kiss of betrayal would come soon.

Pain was in the air later that night, at that last supper. He paused, as he spoke the words to the eleven – mid-bread, mid-wine – the words urgently bursting into the space around the table like crumbs from a ripped loaf: 'My, dear, dear friends, love one another, just as I have loved you.'

They had looked baffled. They knew that commandment, of course they did – it had been passed on, from father to son, from mother to daughter, from family to family for generations, since they had been in the wilderness. They knew it. But he knew that they needed to know these words of new life deep within themselves, digesting them, allowing them to permeate deep within their souls, knowing how he had loved them. Now was too soon, but a day would come…

Before that would come betrayal. Peter protested, of course, but words can slide out, the desire to hide and be hidden can be foundational within the human mind; self-protection, self-preservation run deep. He leaned across to Peter and whispered softly, 'Peter, love one another, just as I have loved you.' The words of denial would come soon.

Jesus looked up at the stars and whispered softly to a silent, sleeping world, unaware of what was to come: 'Love one another, just as I have loved you.'

SUE MORTON

For Sue writing has been a treasure of darkness discovered through many years of trying to recover from ME. She has since travelled the path to ordination and is now minister in six rural churches; she is supported and encouraged by her husband, Mark, her four lovely daughters, and grandson, George.

New Commandments
Week 6: Tuesday

John 14:27

Imagine the peace that Jesus spoke of as being like roots, branches and air. We all choose to put down roots because we wish to build a home for ourselves. We all want to feel that connection, as if we belong. There is a tradition we have at our church that makes everyone feel they are welcome; we share the peace with one another and it means we are starting off our Sunday mornings with kind words and friendly smiles. We like to end the sharing of the peace by singing a hymn that reminds us that his peace is indeed moving in our church. The words of Deep Peace by John Rutter remind us that all we have to do is close our eyes, and search deep within ourselves, to feel the Holy Spirit surrounding us. It feels as if we are getting a massive hug from Jesus. It's only after that, we are filled with confidence about what we must do and we are at peace.

Once we have firmly planted our roots, it's very important to start growing branches. It may take us a while to figure out how to grow in our faith but Jesus already knows and as his followers, he wants us to find a cause bigger than ourselves and be like arrows hitting our targets. In other words, we should stay focused and make a positive change to the wider world in some way. In the final episode of the BBC Television series *The Musketeers* we see the Musketeers under threat and their Garrison bombed. This looks like the end of the

Musketeers because we see a young cadet feeling defeated; he doesn't know how to carry on after such a horrific event. But the captain tells him that the Garrison was only ever 'a place' and that we are 'the Garrison'. This echoes the words of the hymn, 'I am the Church' where we are told how the church is not 'a building' it is 'a people.' Jesus commanded us to ignite the fire in the lives of others so that they too can find this peace for themselves, because wherever we are the spirit of Jesus can be found. After all, it is not called the Good News for nothing.

Let's share the peace that Scripture can bring with kind words and smiles every day. The church is for people to come as they are, regardless of who they are as individuals, and be confronted with the notion that they are good enough and that anything is possible with Jesus. He is the light in the darkness. Loving Jesus is as easy as breathing but obeying him requires us to have complete dedication and commitment to our faith journey and not sit back and enjoy the view. This is not always an easy thing to do because there are times when we feel lost in the mayhem that life brings. Imagine yourself in a labyrinth, many paths to take but not knowing which one to choose.

What we forget to do is listen to the Spirit within and no matter what path we walk down we will ultimately find Jesus waiting for us with unconditional love and understanding. Many writers like Robert Frost in *The Road Not Taken* and Helen Steiner Rice in *The Bend in the Road* have touched upon how we always start off with a plan of how our lives should turn out, but in the end the air sweeps us off in a different direction and we are led to where we need to be. This image reinforces what Christians have always believed. With Jesus at the heart of everything in our lives nothing is too much of a challenge because he is the road map, the compass pointing us in the right direction. Peace means different things to many but the word itself instantly conjures up images of love, acceptance and contentment – that is what the Holy Spirit is all about. We trust that through Jesus everything will turn out the way it's supposed to and the peace that Jesus spoke of will be like growing roots and branches, and breathing air.

KIRSTY WYLLIE

Born and raised in Ayr, Scotland, Kirsty enjoyed a passion for films and theatre from an early age. Brought up in a church-going family, she likes to combine her faith and the dramatic arts together. This has greatly influenced her love of writing, and enabled her to discover her 'niche'.

Holy Week

Introduction
Amy Robinson

We have come to Holy Week, a time to focus on the story of Jesus' last days before the cross. We walk through it day by day in real time. From the day known in some churches as 'Spy Wednesday', when Judas agreed to betray his master for money, to the last supper and the dark agony of the cross; from the strange, eerie quiet of Holy Saturday, to that great burst of light and rejoicing on Easter Sunday for which we have spent all these weeks preparing.

To encounter Jesus in our imaginations in each of these significant moments can be poignant, inspiring, wonderful, unbearable. It's an annual pilgrimage that takes us back to the foot of the cross and the empty grave, and in the familiar scenery, there is always something else to discover for the first time, or to see in a new way. Join us on that journey through the one death that can bring everyone to new life.

Amy is a writer, performance storyteller and ventriloquist, and the children's worker in her benefice. She has written three books about puppetry and storytelling and co-founded the storytelling company Snail Tales. She is the publicity member of the ACW Committee.

Holy Week: Wednesday

Matthew 26: 6-16

There's a crowd gathered around Him, as usual. Simon has taken great care to ensure that only the most important guests have a place at the table with the teacher. You push your way through the onlookers, doing your best to ignore the resentful muttering and scornful glances. The alabaster jar is wrapped securely in a fold of your robe, but you place a protective arm over it, anyway: its contents are worth at least a year's wages.

The swell of conversation dies away as you approach Jesus, and He half-turns towards you. There are gasps of astonishment as you pull the jar from its hiding place. Out of the corner of one eye, you can see the disciples leaning in towards each other, counting on their fingers. You hesitate: this perfume should really have been saved for a burial, but somehow, it feels right.

A heady fragrance fills the room as you crack open the top of the jar, and Jesus inclines His head towards you. Simon frowns as you stretch out your arm, and you try to push aside the angry thoughts you know are being directed at you.

And Jesus waits.

What do you do?

You're standing with the other disciples, crushed together at one side of the room. It's good to see Jesus being treated with respect – for a change – but you wish that Simon had extended the same level of courtesy to His followers, too. It doesn't seem fair that it's always the religious leaders and the Pharisees who get the best seats: they're already puffed up with self-importance.

There's a scuffle at the door, and you see a woman – a woman! – trying to force her way through the throng. She's clutching her robe tightly around her, and there's a look of determination on her face. Your heart sinks more quickly than a stone in the pool of Bethesda: you'd wager your next meal that one of the Pharisees will challenge Jesus if He speaks with the woman. And you know from the gossip of the Passover crowds that the priests are desperate to ensnare Him.

Your jaw drops as the woman produces an alabaster jar and empties the contents over Jesus' head. There is a stunned silence, during which Jesus turns and smiles at the woman, with gentleness in his eyes.

You remember the rich aroma well, from your father's funeral. You also remember how much it cost. Surely Jesus shouldn't be seen to be approving of such wasteful extravagance? The assembled guests are starting to mumble their disapproval, and you clear your throat loudly to attract their attention.

Everyone's eyes are on you as you take a step forwards.

What do you do?

You've spent the past three years following Jesus around the countryside. You've been cold, hungry and unbelievably tired. You've also witnessed astounding miracles: Jesus has healed lepers, raised the dead, fed thousands of people with next to nothing and – a personal favourite – transformed ordinary water into a rich, potent wine.

At first, you were so proud of having been chosen as one of Jesus' special followers. Those first few months were exhilarating: here was a teacher who didn't care about His image, and had a passionate concern for the oppressed. Ordinary people flocked to hear His teaching – and to see the miracles – and you shared their hope that here at last was the Messiah; the One who would rescue the Jewish people.

But gradually, you realised that Jesus showed no inclination to drive out the hated Romans. And while He had frequent verbal clashes with the religious authorities, it didn't appear as if He was going to remove them from their positions of power, either. And slowly, almost imperceptibly, a seed of disappointment took root somewhere deep inside you. You stopped listening so closely to Jesus' words, and became fixated on what you thought He should have said (or done). The kernel of disappointment grew and flourished.

Lately, you've felt frustrated at how you've wasted three years of your life. You've given the best of your time and energy to Jesus, with precious little to show for it. You know you deserve better than this, and so when you overhear the temple staff talking about how to deal with "the teacher problem", you have an idea.

The chief priests seem surprised when you introduce yourself, but for the first time in ages, you feel you're being taken seriously. One of them produces a large money bag, which clinks invitingly as he places it on the table.

"How can we help you?" he says.

What do you do?

You're a twenty-first century believer: you've been following Jesus for a while now. There have been times when it's been absolutely mind-blowingly amazing, but – if you're honest – there have also been times when it's felt like hard work. You wonder if you should be more like that Christian friend who seems to know all the answers and oozes joy through every pore, but doubt, confusion and an overwhelming sense of failure persistently dog your spiritual footsteps. (And in your more lucid moments, you remember that great saints of the past have struggled with these feelings, too.)

So, when something nudges you to respond sacrificially to the needs of others, do you give generously, or do you keep a tight grip on your resources, "just in case"?

When someone else worships in a style that makes you feel uncomfortable, do you give thanks for the rich and varied expressions of worship found in the modern church, or do you sour the atmosphere with judgemental words?

And if your faith feels disappointing, do you acknowledge that God's ways are – mercifully – vastly different from ours, or do you allow resentment and bitterness to throttle your soul, so that you react out of anger rather than a child-like trust?

What do you do?

FIONA LLOYD

Fiona is vice-chair of ACW, and is married with three grown-up children. She is the author of *The Diary of a (trying to be holy) Mum*, (Instant Apostle). Fiona has had stories published in *Woman Alive* and *Writers' News*, and has written articles for *Christian Writer* and *Together Magazine*.

Holy Week: Maundy Thursday

Matthew 26:17-30

Simon is the first to speak. 'Is it me, Lord?'

Next to him, Philip's smile fades. 'It's not me, is it?'

A sudden panic overtakes the room, sweeping all of us with it. *Is it me, Jesus? You can't mean me. I wouldn't ever betray you.*

Then Judas is on his feet. Everyone's eyes turn to him as he walks to Jesus' side, looks down at him. 'Do you mean me?'

For a second they look at each other. Something unspoken passes between them. Then Jesus lowers his gaze. 'Don't play games, Judas.'

Judas nods. He turns to the door and, for the briefest moment, he hesitates. He sways in the doorway: back towards Jesus; forwards towards the darkness outside. I want to call to him – *Don't be an idiot. Come back.* – but I can't seem to find my voice. And in another second the hesitation is over.

He is gone.

It is Jesus who breaks the silence this time. He starts to talk. Not about Judas – not about the one of us who has gone – but about other things. I can't take it in; I don't understand. The room is too hot and the air is too thick and I am drowning in it. I get up and push my way to the door.

In the filthy street, I sink to the floor, lean my head against the cool wall. I am dizzy, dazzled, as if the heavens are crashing down about me. I don't understand anything. Why has Judas left us?

We've all been there, of course. Openly or in private, we've all had our doubts, our moments when we've wondered why we left our widowed mothers, baffled wives and secure jobs for a man we didn't know. Not so long ago it had been me who doubted. The nagging whispers at the edges of my thoughts found strength in the long, dark nights: *What if you are wrong about Jesus? What if he isn't who you need him to be?* One night while the others slept around another fire on another hillside above another town, I'd had enough: too many doubts, too much discomfort. I got up and walked away.

I'd only made it two steps beyond the circle of firelight when the sound of my name halted me.

'Thad?' Judas was getting up, pulling his cloak around him, hurrying after me. 'Where are you going?'

'Home.'

I told him everything then – all I felt and feared.

When I was done, he only shook his head. 'Go if you want to, Thad, but don't pretend to yourself that you don't know who he is. Don't forget you've seen him silence the wind. Don't forget you've seen lepers embraced by their families. Go if you want, but don't pretend you don't know what you're leaving.'

I didn't sleep again that night – didn't lie down with the others. But when dawn broke, I was still there. That was the thing with the twelve of us – we were the ones who stayed. Always.

'Thaddeus?' It is Jesus's voice that calls me this time. 'You OK?'

I open my eyes as he settles on the ground next to me.

'How could he leave us?' I say. 'Judas left everything for you. Why has he gone now?'

Jesus sighs. 'Judas has gone to do what he's chosen to do. We all have choices to make.'

There is something about the way he says it – restrained, sorrowful – that fills me with a sudden terrible certainty. I look at him. 'You're going too, aren't you? That's what you've been trying to tell us.'

'Yes.'

'After everything we've been through? You're leaving us?'

He meets my gaze. 'I have to, Thad.'

'No, you don't.' My voice comes out too loud. 'You don't have to. I know you. You don't have to do anything. You can stop this – whatever it is.'

Jesus lays a hand on my arm. 'If I don't go, I might as well never have come.'

I shake him off. 'What does that even mean? Why don't I ever understand you?' Tears surprise the corners of my eyes. I want to argue with him, reason with him, but the only words I can think of are, 'Don't go.'

'I'll come back for you, Thad. I promise.'

I want to believe him. This man who has never lied to me – I want to trust him.

'There's something you need to know,' I say. 'About me.' I can't look at him. 'There was a time I nearly gave up on you. One night I... I...'

He smiles. 'I know.'

'You don't know. I was going to leave you. It was Judas who...'

'I know, Thad.'

Of course, he does. Of course, he knows.

'That's why I don't understand,' I say. 'Judas believed. He was one of us. And I'm afraid... I'm so afraid that...' I pause, take a deep breath. 'That it could have been me who left tonight. I could have been him.'

'No.' Jesus's voice is sharp. 'You are not him. That's not who you are. You've made your choices – you're here now. That's what matters.'

I look up at the stars. 'He was my friend, Jesus.'

'I know.' There is a catch in Jesus's voice now, a tremble. 'He was my friend too.'

He gets to his feet, turns back to the light spilling from the doorway. 'Come with me, Thad. One more time.'

He is at the door before I call him back. 'Jesus? Are you OK?'

He pauses, but doesn't turn. For a few seconds he is silent, white knuckles gripping the dark wooden door frame. 'I'm here now,' he says at last. 'That's what matters.'

For another minute, I sit in the dark, staring down the path that Judas must have taken. Then, as the heavens begin to fall about me, I follow Jesus back into the light.

CHLOE BANKS
Chloe lives in Devon with her husband and two sons. She started writing for a dare and accidentally forgot to stop. Her short fiction has won a modest handful of prizes and her first novel, *The Art of Letting Go*, was published in 2014. When not trying to get words or toddlers to behave, she can usually be found walking or eating pudding.

Holy Week: Good Friday

Matthew 27:32-37

Some of the most beautiful things in the world have an ugly side. I was recently sent a picture of something that looked as if it belonged in the Christmas section of a plush department store. An array of perfectly spherical red velvet balls were covered with a light dusting of glitter, and held aloft by smooth black stems that emerged from a single varnished branch. Only this was not a table decoration made of wood and velvet, but slime mould at its most picture-perfect. The ugly part of these organisms – if you don't mind the slime – is that they only form their fruiting bodies in times of extreme hunger. The beautiful red baubles in the picture were a sign of starvation, not celebration.

What about the emperor penguin chick, nestling in a feathery pouch above its parent's feet? There's a lovely moment when mum and dad greet each other over the gaping beak of their fuzz-ball offspring. Heads bent together, making a heart shape in the air, they are the very image of matrimonial happiness – or so we think. We can't help seeing a reflection of our own ideals of love in the pair, but the reality of what these birds have been through is even more gruelling than human parenthood. Father penguin has spent all winter sheltering the egg from freezing hurricane-force winds, while mother penguin was feeding at sea. When the chick hatched its parents then played an exhausting game of tag, taking it in turns to walk across the ice and risk being eaten by leopard seals or killer whales so they could catch fish for their chick.

The living world is truly wonderful in so many ways, but the darker side of the picture is never far away. Of course I am projecting values onto organisms that don't share my view of the world; but the reality is that the challenges of life can be seen everywhere you turn. Even the fact that these creatures' experiences remind us of the struggles and pain that haunt our own lives is significant. Creation is groaning (Romans 8:22), and waiting to be rescued.

Enter Jesus, through whom all of creation was made. The King of the universe came to live with us, bringing his great love and wisdom to the human population of first-century Israel. Having spent millennia building a relationship with these people, God finally sent his Son to walk their roads as one of them. The Creator was relating to his creation in a very personal way, and this could have been a totally beautiful picture.

But there is an ugly side of Jesus' story that is so horrifying that it almost obscures the beauty of what he did on Good Friday. Today's passage is brutal: a mind-numbing substance ('wine...mixed with gall') is offered to the prisoner ahead of his excruciating death; the clothes he will not need again are shared out as loot among the soldiers; and the guards are presumably there to stop his friends from either freeing him or giving him a quick death.

Two truths shine out above these stark details. As Jesus stumbles under the burden of the cross, it is given to another man to carry. Simon the bystander is pressed into service to keep the show on the road. He has no choice in the matter, but in a sense his sacrifice mirrors what Jesus is about to do. He takes on another's load, when it had become too much for him to carry.

The other truth is in the sign. Ancient Greek didn't distinguish between upper and lower case for names, but the translation here conveys the disrespect the soldiers may have felt for their prisoners. The words themselves were true, but they were far short of the full truth. Jesus is my King too, and the King of every other human being. He is the King of the slime mould, the penguins, and every other living thing on earth. The earth itself, the moon, stars, and galaxies beyond are also part of his realm.

The beauty in the events of Good Friday is that Jesus died to redeem all of creation. This was all part of his plan to rescue us from pain and death, and to save all of creation from its trials and the destruction wreaked on it by those who were supposed to serve and preserve it. We have been promised resurrection, and a restored and renewed creation. What things will look like in a physical, renewed, creation – I don't know. The cycles of life and death cannot go on if death itself is ended. Perhaps we might get slime mould fruiting bodies without the threat of starvation, but we'll just have to find out. The details are trivial compared with the truth that the rescue itself will actually happen.

The effects of the cataclysmic events surrounding the death and resurrection of Jesus Christ can already be seen rippling out into the world, for those who care to look. Human lives are changed for the better, even if their day-to-day existence is still incredibly tough. Those changes can also have an effect on the non-human parts of creation. When people come to understand what creation is for, and who it belongs to, they can learn to do their job as images of God on earth properly. They can begin to serve and preserve the earth rather than using up its fruitfulness as fast as possible. These things are only whispers of what is to come, but they give me hope for the future redemption of all creation.

So that ugly day nearly 2,000 years ago is called 'good' because of what it achieved. Jesus' brutal death on the cross was part of a series of events that will set his people and the rest of creation free from sin and death forever. I can choose to dwell on the beauty of Jesus' death because the events we're reading about today were not the end of the story – Easter Sunday beckons.

DR RUTH BANCEWICZ
Ruth is a Senior Research Associate at The Faraday Institute for Science and Religion, working on the positive interaction between science and faith. After studying genetics at Aberdeen and Edinburgh Universities, she worked for the UK-based professional group Christians in Science. She has written several books, and blogs at scienceandbelief.org.

Holy Week: Holy Saturday

Matthew 27: 62-66

We wait.

Not like we wait for a bus or a train. Or in a queue in a shop. In normal circumstances, we understand the end of our waiting. The bus will come. The train will arrive. We will find ourselves at the head of the queue and the shop assistant will serve us. Then we will move on. But this is different waiting. Today we cannot move on. We must simply wait.

We can, of course, choose where to wait. Perhaps we can sit in the corner of Pilate's courts and hear the sound of sandals slapping against the stone floors. A gaggle of agitated men hurries into view. It is Shabbat, but they have laid aside the constraints of their own rules to bring the thought that torments them to the man whose power constrains their own. 'That imposter… that deceiver… that liar,' they cry, barely noticing the paradox. 'That liar said…' And Pilate, perhaps still bewildered by his own encounter with Jesus, is drawn into their disquiet. The men rush away, anxious to get their guard to the imposter's tomb. But they cannot rest easy, even on Shabbat. Pilate returns to his chambers and to his own thoughts. And we are left to wait.

Perhaps we can linger with the guards at Jesus' grave. They too are apprehensive men. The garden location is pleasant enough, the weather warm. But they listen for the scrape of sandals on the dry, rough, stony soil. They

214 – New Life

strain to hear whispers. They glance above the silver-green branches of aging olive trees to the safety of the city walls. Their fear casts shadows over their conversation. Will these followers of Jesus come in force or stealth to seize the body? Behind them the tomb is as silent as... well, as a grave. But there are rumours. This Jesus was a prophet; the Messiah, some said. He promised to rise from the dead. From time to time, they glance nervously around, afraid that the real danger lies in the darkness behind. Nothing can disturb the dead, they joke. But the laughter, like the hillside, is hollow.

The hardest place to sit is with the followers of Jesus. That too is an anxious and fearful place. But as we enter their story, the door is locked behind us. If soldiers come, there will be no escape. Now we are hemmed in with these men and women who loved and have lost Jesus; caught up in their thoughts, feeling their emotion, sharing their conversation.

In truth, we should pack our belongings into bags and creep out of Jerusalem. We have seen Jesus on the cross and we know that he is dead. We have watched Joseph lay the body in the grave and felt the shudder of the stone as it came to rest across the gaping hole of the tomb. We should say goodbye to our companions of the last three years and return home. People will talk, but they will forget once we settle on the seat in the tax booth, or take our place in the fishing boat. But we wait in Jerusalem, no more than a few hundred metres from the tomb. This black day we need to be together, bearing grief, finding consolation in not being alone.

Talk stutters into life. More than once Jesus spoke of coming back to life. How could that ever be possible?

We hardly believed he would die and, whether we like it or not, that has been fulfilled. He even told us how he would die. And when. How could he be so right about dying and yet now we hesitate to believe him? Are we to abandon his prophecies? We have been proved wrong about Jesus more times than we choose to remember. Dare we hope that what he said will truly be true?

No-one moves. Our sandals lie discarded at the door; our feet unwashed in mourning. We sit looking at each other like fools. Nobody believes it. Except that... Jesus said it. He had restored Lazarus and that girl, the daughter of Jairus, to life. And there was the young man at Nain. Could Jesus really step out of death and walk back into our lives?

We laugh at ourselves and then stumble into exhausted silence. The interlude breaks and we talk of the things Jesus did. We laugh again and some of us cry. We recite his sayings and retell his tales of sheep and sowers, and buried coins and hidden treasure, and then... the light in the room brightens and we glance at the sun as it dips beneath the head of the window. 'Three days,' says someone. 'The third day,' I say.

We stay where we are. Waiting for Saturday's dusk to die. Praying that Jesus is indeed the way, the truth, the life. Hoping beyond hope that the Son will rise on Sunday. We cannot move on until we know. And if he does step out of death, where will he take us?

RONALD CLEMENTS
Ronald Clements is a fulltime freelance writer. His books include *Lives from a Black Tin Box* and *In Japan the Crickets*

Cry, missionary biographies set in Africa and Asia. He has written for feature films and written/directed TV documentaries, as well as producing Christian apologetic and resource material. www.ronaldclements.com

Holy Week: Easter Sunday

John 20:11-18

Woman, why the tears?

They've taken my Lord away.
Where have they put him?

Woman, why the tears?
Who are you looking for?

Sir, have you carried him away?
Tell me and I'll get him.

Mary.

In a moment, she knows
Running towards him with joy,
Teacher!

Don't hold onto me

I've not yet gone to the Father.

Go to my brothers

Tell them:

To my Father I'm ascending

To your Father

To my God

To your God.

She went, rejoicing,

I have seen the Lord!

We weep, not understanding. Why? Why did he have to die? Why is she now gone? How will we carry on?

When someone dies, we experience the feelings Mary felt at the tomb where Jesus lay. For my family, the call came when we were visiting Minnesota, the first time in years the four of us travelled together from London to my childhood home. When my husband got off the phone, he shared news that made our hearts race – his mum had fallen in the night and cracked some vertebrae, and the prognosis wasn't good. Although Nicholas made it back to England to say goodbye before she died, life would never be the same. For the first time, our children experienced the death of a loved one, and their grief would erupt or leak out at surprising moments. My assurance to them was simple but profound: 'Grandma is now with Jesus. She's not in pain and is filled with joy. She lives again!'

Over many months, my regular need to comfort my children as they mourned their grandmother made me realise anew how much hope I find in the tenets of the Christian faith, which can be expressed simply. See how much truth can be packed into a few words: 'Jesus died for my sins, and he rose again. He's alive!' Or in a well-known children's song: 'Jesus loves me, this I know, for the Bible tells me so.' Or, fittingly for today, the Easter acclamation: 'Christ is risen! He is risen indeed! Alleluia!'

Alleluia! He is alive! We might exclaim those words with joy, or through gritted teeth, or somewhere in between. I think of the late Rob Lacey, and how we'd chat about what he wanted to call his memoir of his cancer journey and God's faithfulness through it. He'd say, 'I know! The title should be, "Halle-*&^%-luia!" Think the publishers would let that through?' With wry humour, he affirmed the truths that God is faithful, and Christ is risen, but at times in our broken world we must praise God while the tears fall.

Imagine the confusion Mary must have felt as she lingered near the tomb, trying to figure out not only why Jesus had to die but where his body had gone. All the joy she had felt earlier in his presence drained away with her tears. Now she was confused, disheartened, disappointed. Not only were her hopes and dreams lying in a heap of ashes, but even her beloved Jesus' body had disappeared.

But with one word, her confusion vanished and joy flooded her soul. With only one word from Jesus she experienced astounded relief – the One who called her by name was alive! His body wasn't lying dead in the tomb for he was with her, speaking new life to her. He lived!

And that is the amazing truth that we shout from the rooftops and in our churches on Resurrection Sunday: Christ is risen! He is risen indeed! Alleluia! What difference do these few words make? Quite simply, everything.

For through them we have the sure hope of eternal life. We know that our mothers and brothers and friends who love Jesus will live forever with him, and with us. Saying goodbye to them when they die cracks our heart but doesn't break it, because we know that God will follow through on his promises of life in the kingdom of heaven. And there no longer will we have to praise God through gritted teeth or falling tears, for no longer will we even experience pain or tears or crying our mourning or death. The old order will have passed away and the new one will have come.

So on this Easter Sunday, whether you exclaim that Christ is risen with joy reverberating through your being, or you do so while sensing you're in a spiritual winter and that God feels very far away, hold onto the awe-inspiring promises of life in the kingdom of God through the risen Son. He comes to us and speaks our names, and we rise from our grief in joy.

Christ is risen! He is risen indeed! Alleluia!

Prayer

Father God, you sent Jesus to die for me, to wipe away my long account of wrongdoing. But your Son didn't stay in the tomb, because he rose again and lives with us now! You have given me not only the gift of eternal life, but Jesus and the Holy Spirit dwelling within me; you bring me comfort when I'm struggling and shower me with joy and love. Give me your sure hope of new life, and help me to share this truth in love to those whom I meet. Lord Jesus, you are risen! I rejoice! Alleluia!

AMY BOUCHER PYE
Amy is the author of the award-winning *Finding Myself in Britain* and the BRF Lent book on forgiveness, *The Living Cross*. She has an MA in Christian spirituality, runs the Woman Alive book club and writes devotional articles for several publications, including *Our Daily Bread*. Find her at amyboucherpye.com.

EDITORS

AMY ROBINSON

Amy Robinson is a writer, performance storyteller and ventriloquist, and the children's worker in her benefice. She has written three books about puppetry and storytelling, published by Kevin Mayhew, and provides scripts and materials for GenR8, a Cambridgeshire charity running Christian assemblies and events in schools. She co-founded the storytelling company *Snail Tales*, with which she still writes and performs. In her spare time, she writes poetry and makes attempts at novels. She lives in a rectory in Suffolk with the rector, two children, two guinea pigs and too many puppets to count.

WENDY H. JONES

Wendy H. Jones is the author of the highly successful, award winning crime series *The DI Shona McKenzie Mysteries*. She also writes the *Fergus and Flora Mysteries* and the *Cass Claymore* series. After having a career in the Military she moved into Academia, where she wrote for academic publications and textbooks. She has had extensive marketing training throughout her career. After a period of illness she moved back to her native Scotland where she settled in Dundee. This led to her career as an author. She is the founder of *Crime at the Castle*, Scotland's newest Crime Festival, presents *Wendy's Book Buzz* Radio Show, on MearnsFM, and is a partner in *Equipped to Write*, a training and coaching company.

FIND OUT MORE

Visit ACW online at
www.christianwriters.org.uk

Connect with ACW on twitter at

twitter.com/ACW1971

MORE BOOKS

The ACW Advent book
will be released in November 2018.